Optimizing Corporate Portfolio Management

Aligning Investment Proposals with Organizational Strategy

Inside of Book Endorsements

"*Optimizing Corporate Portfolio Management* is a refreshing treatise on an age-old problem—how to allocate the resources across the firm. It makes a very coherent argument for aligning the allocation decisions across financial, strategic and risk objectives. The reader is guaranteed to be given a fresh look and a broader perspective on how to tackle this very challenging organization. A must read at the top of the organization!!!"

David J. Reibstein
Professor of Marketing,
The Wharton School—University of Pennsylvania

"Finally a book that delivers against an ambitious corporate portfolio management premise. A compelling solution backed by an unparalleled framework, pragmatic implementation steps and case studies. A must have for all organizational leaders trying to maximize the value of their corporate investments."

San Retna
Chair, Enterprise Portfolio Management Council
Principal, TransformAction

"Pragmatic and full of real-life examples...a must-read for anyone involved with or practicing portfolio management."

Piyush Sanghani
Director, Portfolio Management,
Trans Union LLC

"This book will be very helpful to any executive who wants to improve their organization's resource allocation processes and make smarter investment decisions. Sanwal writes with the perspective of someone who has been 'in the trenches' and provides clear guidance on the realities of implementing rigorous processes in the real world."

Don N. Kleinmuntz, PhD
Research Professor of Policy and Management, University of Southern California
Executive Vice President and CFO, Strata Decision Technology, LLC

"Progressive thinking on a staid business problem. A well-thought, useful framework for corporate investment managers everywhere—the professed mountain is not insurmountable."

Ronald D. Balzan
Vice President - Business Analysis & Treasurer
AIG Consumer Finance Group, Inc.

"Allocating capital to new projects and opportunities has a greater effect on strategy than perhaps any other process in an organization. And still, it remains one of the least understood processes in management. Anand Sanwal's in-depth examination surfaces insights on how to link capital allocation to strategic planning. His book provides not only a detailed description of the complexities of the problem, but practitioner oriented advice for what to do about it."

Clark Gilbert
Former Harvard Business School Professor
Co-author of "From Resource Allocation to Strategy"

"Anand Sanwal's new book does a great job of developing and explaining new approaches to portfolio management. I especially value the emphasis on the need for good metrics to close the learning loop on portfolio decisions."

Paul Farris
Landmark Communications Professor of Business Administration
Darden School, University of Virginia

Portfolio Management was one of the breakthroughs of modern finance and its application to the Corporation's activities shows much promise—however, today it is much more art than science. Anand Sanwal's book is a significant contribution to turning CPM into a science.

Martin Curley
Senior Principal Engineer and Global Director IT Innovation and Research
Intel Corporation

"*Optimizing Corporate Portfolio Management* articulates a discipline and strategy that will significantly benefit large- and middle-market companies alike. Anand Sanwal avoids simplistic one size fits all approaches which have become commonplace in discussions of portfolio management to deliver keen, no-nonsense insights that will strengthen your organization."

Rajesh Shah
Executive Vice President,
MS International, Inc.

Optimizing Corporate Portfolio Management

Aligning Investment
Proposals with
Organizational Strategy

ANAND SANWAL

BICENTENNIAL
1807
WILEY
2007
BICENTENNIAL

John Wiley & Sons, Inc.

Library of Congress Cataloging-in-Publication Data
Sanwal, Anand, 1973-
    Optimizing corporate portfolio management : aligning investment proposals with organizational strategy / Anand Sanwal.
        p. cm.
    Includes index.
    ISBN: 978-0-470-12688-2 (cloth : alk. paper)
    1. Corporations—Finance. 2. Portfolio management. I. Title.
HG4011.S324 2007
658.15'2—dc22

Dedication

To Mom, Dad, Srilekha, Indu, Meenu, and Alex

Contents

About the Web Site

As a purchaser of this book, *Optimizing Corporate Portfolio Management: Aligning Investment Proposals with Organizational Strategy,* you have access to the supporting Web site:

www.wiley.com/go/sanwal

The Web site contains:

- **Survey to Analyze Your Organization's CPM Capabilities and Readiness**. This survey targeted at potential CPM discipline leaders gauges your beliefs about your organization's current processes and behavior as it relates to CPM. The survey ends with a scoring framework which can be used to prescriptively understand where your organization stands and what you should focus on as you embark on building a CPM capability within your organization.

- **High Level Practitioner Survey.** This survey for distribution among potential CPM stakeholders within your organization aims to understand the following:
  - Your organization's familiarity and receptivity to the CPM discipline
  - What your organization has done in order to enable CPM
  - What your organization's strengths are with respect to CPM
  - What the development areas of your organization are with reference to CPM

- **Practitioner's Presentation.** This document contains graphics and exhibits that will be useful to practitioners looking to generate support for implementing or enhancing their Corporate Portfolio Management discipline.

Foreword

Several years ago our CEO, Kenneth Chenault asked me "How do we know we are allocating our resources to the best investments?" This seemingly simple question set us off on the path to the concept we call at American Express, Investment Optimization (IO), or Corporate Portfolio Management (CPM).

While it is common practice for companies to spend significant time on the allocation of capital, few companies do comprehensive reviews on the allocation of precious expense dollars. At American Express, this began with a simple idea; all discretionary expense dollars whether marketing, sales force and technology investments need to compete for these same dollars. IO gives you the ability to evaluate the countless investment opportunities to determine which opportunities deserve the marketing, capital, or human resources.

As a company practicing the CPM discipline, we utilize and benefit from CPM across our organization. It is one of the most powerful disciplines the company has adopted. While the initial concept of IO initiated in Finance, it is now entrenched in the company's Strategic Planning process. Our business leaders have seen the benefits on the bottom line: investments yielding greater returns as CPM helps allocate resources to the best investment opportunities. The results have been outstanding with strong growth in investment spending since 2001.

The final stage, and one we consider the most powerful, is closing the loop. IO is not simply about projections but feeding back actual results to compare how we have performed.

This is the IO strategy at American Express and I hope you find this an interesting read.

Gary L. Crittenden
Former Executive Vice President and Chief Financial Officer
American Express

Preface

To describe what makes this book different, it may be useful to tell you what you should and should not expect from the text you have before you. Most importantly, it is worth understanding that this book is written from the perspective of a practitioner for fellow practitioners.

This book is not the presentation of corporate portfolio management (CPM) as the solution to all that ails your organization. If you are looking for a silver bullet or black box that will tell you how to more efficiently manage your organization's portfolio of investments, I suggest you stop reading now. There is no magic 2×2 matrix, scorecard, process map, or Six Sigma way to an optimal corporate investment portfolio. CPM does not consist of sanitized, immediately gratifying one- or two-dimensional messages about sustainable competitive advantage and organizational excellence. It is not an idealistic or impractical framework or process that neglects to consider organizational constraints, politics, and behaviors in favor of a gimmick.

Assuming your interest is in getting your hands dirty and investing time to make CPM happen, this book is a pragmatic guide to enabling the implementation of CPM in your organization. It details a practical capability that works only when organizational behavior and process are aligned. CPM is rigorous and data driven. When you do not have data, you are often forced to make bold, emotional, intuitive, decibel-driven decisions. CPM is no less bold and is undoubtedly a large change-management effort. And by leveraging data and the inherent logic and reason that data and analytics provide, it lets substance prevail over style. Enabling CPM requires the will of a marathoner, not a sprinter. It calls for time, effort, resources, and patience, but the benefits are significant and will create the sustainable competitive advantage and organizational excellence you seek. CPM is counter to many current trends and corporate fashions. An article in the October 2006 *McKinsey Quarterly* appropriately cautioned that "executives should eschew simplistic organizational solutions . . . popular techniques such as management incentives and key performance indicators (KPIs) are strikingly ineffective."

Advice from "experts on organizational performance often fall into either of two traps. Some of these authorities fail to give the full picture because they assume that companies already have a number of complementary building blocks in place and therefore systematically overestimate the impact of a single practice. Others have a preference for one big, visible intervention they regard as more effective than a combination of less dramatic initiatives," contends the same *McKinsey Quarterly* article. A CPM capability requires that building blocks be put into place in order for CPM to be successful, and these building blocks, in and of themselves, will provide smaller, less dramatic interim wins to the organization. When these components of the foundation are in place and CPM is practiced in the organization, dramatic results can be expected. This book talks about how the requisite behavioral and process building blocks can be put into place for long-term CPM success.

This book does not explain why CPM is important. The assumption is that you have already realized, even superficially, the value of CPM and picked this book up because you are now looking for a practical guide on how to implement it.

This book does not present theories that can be applied to optimize a portfolio. Linear optimization, real options analysis, predictive markets, Monte Carlo simulation, and others are all interesting and valuable applications. These can and should be leveraged if and when your organization has a well-running CPM discipline in place and when the information and data inputs into and emerging from your CPM efforts are credible. Applying these tools prematurely in the hopes that they will uncover or resolve other deficiencies in your approach to CPM is not useful. Although many organizations do attempt this, they are ultimately confusing activity with progress or, in some instances, looking for a portfolio management panacea that does not exist. I will present a brief overview of these frameworks and tools, but there are many robust resources out there (books, academicians, etc.) that can be tapped into when your organization reaches a level of sophistication that requires application of these tools and theories.

This book does not provide a universal resource allocation framework or a generalized one-size-fits-all group of metrics or a scorecard to evaluate an organization's investments. The idea of a general corporate resource allocation framework is a fallacy. Because organizations have different types of investments, priorities, risk tolerances, strategies, and goals, methods to optimize CPM are organization-specific, and even within a single organization, one generalized resource allocation framework will generally be insufficient. Ultimately, frameworks and scorecards are not enablers of CPM—they can be useful tools to aid in ongoing evaluation and optimization of the corporate portfolio.

This book does not suggest a technology-based cure-all approach to CPM. Although many consultants and software vendors would have you believe their tools are key to optimizing your organization's portfolio, their claims are most often spurious. Technology can help with the aggregation, reporting of, and analysis of your organization's portfolio, but there is no technology tool that can optimize your organization's portfolio for you. In fact, despite the emergence of myriad project and portfolio management (PPM) tools, most, to this point, are glorified data aggregation and reporting tools. Technology, thoughtfully applied, can help you enable the process with greater efficiency, accountability, and transparency, but it is not the solution or even one of the most essential components of the solution.

This book touches on some of the previously mentioned elements, but its main intention is to provide practitioners with a guide to building a robust CPM capability within their organizations. This practitioner's guide has come together utilizing:

- A pragmatic and proven CPM discipline, one that I, along with numerous talented colleagues, have had the opportunity to build at American Express (referred to as "investment optimization" within American Express). Elements of the approach have patent-pending status (U.S. Application No. 11/256,340), and it has been successfully utilized to generate results that have received significant attention from external third parties. The discipline has occasioned significant interest from external think tanks and has served as the basis for presentations I have given to the members of the CFO Executive Board, Corporate Strategy Board, Controllers' Leadership Roundtable, Gartner, Enterprise Portfolio Management Council, Beyond Budgeting Roundtable, as well as direct presentations I have given on the topic to individual corporations. The discipline has also garnered external acclaim, having received two *Baseline* ROI awards (sponsored by *Baseline Magazine*) including both the award for innovation and the overall grand prize award. The simple yet effective software application underlying the discipline was also recognized as one of the *InfoWorld* Top 100 applications of 2005.

- Conversations with nearly 100 corporate practitioners and subject-matter experts who have graciously provided their insights on the processes they have employed, along with the challenges, successes, and insights they have acquired in their development of a CPM discipline. The wisdom imparted by these individuals has been invaluable in the development and further refinement of the CPM discipline outlined within this book.

You will also notice that this book takes a decidedly financial view of CPM because the dollar (or any currency) is the one finite resource that all areas of a company (whether a business unit or specific functional area such as IT, operations, marketing, etc.) understand and that they are faced with managing and optimizing. There are other resources (personnel, plant assets, etc.) that can be collected as part of your CPM discipline and that can be optimized, but financial metrics present us with a universally understandable language across organizations.

Critics will argue that taking such a financial perspective fails to consider an investment or a portfolio's strategic impact or "strategic-ness." This is most definitely not the case. A well-run corporate portfolio is actually the manifestation of an organization's strategy. For example, if your corporate vision is to retain and delight customers and your investments are all made to acquire new customers, there is a lack of alignment between your stated strategy and your true strategy. In this case, your corporate strategy has been reduced to words on a wall or in a well-designed PowerPoint document. Where you allocate money (e.g., your corporate portfolio) is your strategy. Take this simple but often-occurring exchange within many organizations.

General Manager: "Your investment suggests we spend $1 million a year for the next five years, yet there is no resulting financial benefit from this investment. Why should we do it?"

Investment Owner: "We need to do this investment for strategic reasons."

Strategy is often an excuse investment owners use as the justification of last resort or when an investment owner does not want to think about why to do an investment. In essence, strategy is the reason often cited when the benefits of a particular idea cannot be articulated in a more lucid manner.

Because the organizations looking to develop a CPM practice may be at different levels of evolution, there may be elements of the book that you may not find applicable, insofar as you may have already proceeded past those steps in the process. Nevertheless, it is my expectation that you will find some element of this guide useful as you construct or enhance your CPM capabilities.

TERMINOLOGY

I have tried very hard to keep corporate and management consultant jargon to a minimum, but I fear that despite my best efforts to prevent this, many of these words have crept into the recesses of my brain, therefore, somewhat unintentionally; they rear their ugly heads at times. I apologize in advance for leveraging such terms, but at times, discussion of this leading-edge topic and my domain expertise of it required synergistic use of these terms in order to syndicate and socialize these concepts. Terrible.

Jargon aside, I have also attempted to minimize the use of technical terms and acronyms throughout the book. Still, there are a few notable ones that are used throughout for the purposes of clarity and brevity.

CPM is most obviously the acronym for corporate portfolio management. It is used to describe both the capability and a means of managing an organization as well as the actual portfolio under consideration.

The term "organization" is used throughout the book to refer to an entire corporation or enterprise. It also refers to any type of organization, whether for profit or not. Conversely, it can refer to a specific subsegment of the organization to which you may be trying to bring a CPM discipline. For instance, if you are the general manager of a product group or the CFO of a region or the CIO in charge of IT, your respective organization would be defined as the product group, region, or IT organization, respectively.

CPM is about optimizing resource allocation, so it is important to understand that a resource is any finite asset (tangible or intangible) that a company has to expend to make an investment happen. It may be money, people, manufacturing capacity, or time, to name a few specifics. Money is the main resource discussed in this book in that it is universal across all organizations.

"Investment" is also used throughout the book; most generally, it refers to any discretionary initiative requiring or competing for resources. As you will see in subsequent discussion, many organizations too narrowly define what a discretionary investment is and attribute too much of their operating expenditures and even capital expenditures to what would be called business as usual or steady state investments.

CBA is the acronym for cost/benefit analysis, which your organization may create when evaluating an investment idea. Many organizations also refer to these analyses as models or financial models. CBA can and should include nonfinancial benefits and costs as well. Additionally, the term "model," while sounding grand, is generally a misnomer that overstates the sophistication actually being employed. In my experience, many Excel creations have often been disguised as—or rather promoted unnecessarily to—"model" status when they are really just glorified input or data-entry sheets. Additionally, I want to ensure that there is a distinction between CBAs and driver-based models, which are also discussed.

Driver-based models really deserve the term "model," because they attempt to distill an investment's behavior down into distinct drivers, which, when calculated, actually drive the behavior of an investment.

For example, if we are considering a direct-mail investment a CBA might indicate that I am expecting $1 million in revenue and the cost of the direct mail is $200,000 for a pre-tax profit of $800,000. A driver-based model, however, would instead ask questions about the underlying drivers to arrive at the financials and look something like this (*note:* this is a very simple example):

$$\text{Number of mail pieces dropped} = 400{,}000$$

$$\text{Expected response rate} = 1.0\%$$

$$\text{Expected revenue/customer} = \$250$$

$$\text{Cost per piece of direct mail} = \$0.50/\text{piece}$$

Therefore,

$$\text{Revenue} = 400{,}000 \text{ pieces} \times 1\% \text{ responding} \times \$250 = \$1{,}000{,}000$$

$$\text{Cost} = 400{,}000 \text{ pieces} \times \$0.50/\text{piece} = \underline{\$200{,}000}$$

$$\text{Pre-tax Profit} = \$800{,}000$$

From the preceding example, you can draw the general conclusion that a sufficiently robust driver-based model (one that considers strategic, financial, and risk returns) is also a CBA but not every CBA is a driver-based model.

Of course, given that this book is about CPM, which is inherently tied to financial returns, I may use widely known financial terms such as those in the following list. I will not go into an explanation of these. As there are several excellent resources (online and offline) that can expound on these in a much better fashion. These terms include the following:

- EBIT—earnings before interest and taxes
- EBITDA—earnings before interest, taxes, depreciation, and amortization
- IRR—internal rate of return
- NPV—net present value
- PTI—pre-tax income
- ROI—return on investment
- Payback
- Software capitalization

Note: Given the rapid pace at which CPM is evolving, practitioners can continue to learn about current CPM news, ideas, and practices at http://www.corporateportfoliomanagement.org.

Anand Sanwal
asanwal@corporateportfoliomanagement.org

Acknowledgments

This book would not have been possible without the support and insights of many individuals. Before acknowledging any particular individual, I must recognize and thank American Express, where I was given the opportunity and freedom to learn about and help to develop a best-in-class corporate portfolio management practice. At American Express, we refer to the company's corporate portfolio management (CPM) discipline as investment optimization (IO). Undoubtedly, American Express is an innovator in the area of CPM, as the company realized the importance of this discipline five years ago, long before it came into vogue and significantly before a veritable industry formed around the practice of CPM. American Express invested considerable resources in making IO a reality, and today, after the efforts of many people, American Express's CPM discipline has become part of the company's DNA, impacting investment decision making across the company—whether it is within marketing, IT, operations, product development, or any other area.

Despite the company's being far ahead in regard to its CPM capability, American Express has always sought to learn from others, and it is this openness that has led to many of my conversations with practitioners at other companies. Furthermore, the company has always been willing to share its best practices in CPM with others in the hopes that by doing so, the sophistication of and the discussion about CPM would increase, ultimately benefiting all involved in the discussion. Not every company is willing to share and be so open about what could be considered a competitive practice and advantage, and for this reason, I owe a debt of gratitude to the company.

I am also very indebted to the many people I have had the opportunity to work with and learn from at American Express. First and foremost, I need to thank American Express's CFO, Gary Crittenden, for graciously agreeing to write the Foreword to this book and for his steadfast support and sponsorship of IO. Alan Gallo and Vince Nerlino both provided significant sponsorship and resources for IO within the organization, and they allowed me and the IO team considerable freedom to develop and refine our portfolio management discipline at American Express over time. For their support, I am also very grateful. Beyond the senior-level sponsorship the IO initiative has received, I have been fortunate to work with many talented individuals at American Express who have helped in the formulation of many of the ideas in this book, who have helped me edit it along the way, or who have had to hear me talk on any and every occasion about CPM and how every company should be doing this and how it could change how organizations work.

I would also like to thank my team at American Express, the investment optimization and strategic business analysis group, who continuously amaze me with their intelligence, drive, and insights and whose efforts have moved American Express's CPM efforts ahead. The specific people on my team, now and in the past who deserve mention include Amith Nirgunarthy, Anar Kothari, Arun Pandurangi, Ben Pegler, Chandrima Dhanuka, Dominic Paniccia, Evelyn Serrano, Gary Musselwhite, Gaurav Mehra, George Robinson, Jane Hsu, Karen Klein, Lina Zheng, Rahul Ramesh, Ritesh Sharma, Robert Johansen, Sidharth Bansal, Vladimir Vilensky, and Yan Hu. Let me also thank many other American Express colleagues whom I have had the opportunity to work with on the company's IO efforts, including Joanne Leong, Chris Riegger, Chris Stanley, Gloria Suen, James Tsantes, John Kakascik, Michael Haran, Patrick Burke, Pat Leong, Ranjan Lall, Rob Finkelstein, Rob Pereless, Samantha Fliegler, Scott Peterson, Steve Mackay, Tracey Ingram, and Zach Wasserman. Finally, there are many other colleagues and friends I have met through American Express and have had the pleasure of working with who also deserve some thanks, as they have played some role in the writing of this book. Sometimes that role was listening to me worry about not being sure whether I was ever going to finish it, sometimes it was a conversation which expanded my thinking about CPM, sometimes it was actually reading excerpts and telling me what they thought and many times it was a kind word or a helping hand before an important meeting or deadline. So thanks to Chitra Narasimhan, Jay Shah, Dudley Brundige, Alex Hopwood, Bernadette Murphy, Milind Karnik, Ajit Sequeira, Sandeep Arora, Jaime Croake, Jacinta Sheahan, Vikram Nangia, Mark Rosen, Rita Berk, Peggy Cowherd, Marva Tinglin-Mason, Rosa Baez, Mike Applegate, Corey Barak, and Toby Prince. There were so many people within Corporate Planning and Analysis at American Express who have helped in developing the ideas presented in the book that you hold in your hand, so I apologize if I have inadvertently missed someone.

Beyond the folks at American Express, I am indebted to the many practitioners and subject-matter experts who helped to refine and broaden my thinking on CPM. The CFO Executive Board's Eisha Armstrong and Roisin Ryan who provided me with considerable research and numerous introductions to thought leaders at other companies, deserve special thanks. No request I ever made of them (and I made quite a few) has taken more than one day to fulfill. Their responsiveness, intelligence, and professionalism are remarkable, and I am very appreciative of their help. Piyush Sanghani of TransUnion, Michael Menke and Kevin Yorks of HP, David Wells of the State of Oregon's Department of Human Services, and Bill Bien of Cisco provided me with invaluable insights and gave of their time for the book's case studies. I learned a great deal from each of them and appreciate their organizations' sharing their progressive CPM practices with others.

Let me also thank my friends from Wharton and Penn, who have heard me drone on and on about CPM and who always encourage me even though they worry about my obsession with this topic. And last, but certainly not least, I must thank my wife, Sri, and the rest of my family for putting up with me and my constant talk about the book during the past few months. Without their support, patience, and understanding, this book would never have been possible.

CHAPTER 1

Overview of Corporate Portfolio Management

Notwithstanding noble efforts to do so, most organizations continue to fail in aligning their discretionary investment expenditures with the organization's financial, strategic, and risk objectives. The decision-making process in most organizations remains heavily politicized, intuition led, and silo prone. Corporate strategy groups and myriad consultants have recognized and opined on the pitfalls and perils of these decision-making processes and silos, and their proposed solutions, whether they take the form of a series of metrics, technology platforms, or frameworks, have been highly ineffective—all sizzle, no steak. The consequence of these codified business rituals and failed attempts at "solutions" has been a continuous stream of subpar decisions on individual investments. And when discrete investments are not being successfully evaluated, an overall view of these investments in their totality—as a portfolio of opportunities—is only a mirage for many organizations.

Corporate portfolio management (CPM) brings the goal of defining a portfolio strategy for discretionary investments into focus, and given an appropriate level of commitment, it can make a previously opaque process lucid. It is an organizational capability and strategy that considers finite resource availability in a manner that enables a company to optimize its portfolio across the myriad investment opportunities available to it. When successfully executed, CPM provides companies with an *ongoing* rigorous data-driven capability for the evaluation, prioritization, selection, and monitoring of individual investment opportunities. More importantly, it allows these individual decisions to be aggregated into an organizational portfolio that can create competition for finite resources among these investment opportunities. Ultimately, this leads to optimization of the organization's portfolio across strategic, financial, and risk objectives. The flexibility of CPM also enables mid-cycle investment and portfolio appraisals as well as adjustments based on changing objectives or market conditions.

In an organization that has certain established inbuilt processes, CPM can appear to be a daunting task, given the monolithic proportions of some organizational portfolios. The task can be made more manageable by understanding that the corporate portfolio, in most instances, actually consists of many mini-portfolios, which compose the overall enterprise portfolio. And it is actually the optimization of these mini-portfolios that can drive total company portfolio optimization. These corporate mini-portfolios are often organizationally specific, but common mini-portfolios and the example investment decisions that need to be considered include

- **Lines of business (LOB).** Customer acquisition investment in one LOB versus a customer retention investment in another LOB?
- **Regional or geographic markets.** Invest in Europe or Asia? Brazil or Argentina? New York or Chicago?
- **Product groups.** Additional marketing for product 1 or new product features for product 2?
- **Information technology.** Disaster recovery project or new product platform?
- **Advertising and promotion.** Direct mail or online pay-per-click advertising?
- **Innovation and R&D.** Innovative product idea or innovative marketing idea?
- **Capital assets.** Expansion of existing facility or investment in new facility?

The foregoing are only examples, which will be explored in greater detail throughout the book. The investment decision is not binary in most instances, which accounts in part for the difficulty organizations experience in making portfolio management decisions.

Investment selection within these mini-portfolios can be complicated by the fact that they have different risk reward characteristics and they frequently utilize different metrics. This complexity is readily handled by a well-conceived CPM capability, and it is a source of CPM's power as it allows the organization or components of the organization to look at their business in a more rigorous but still familiar way.

WHY IS CPM IMPORTANT?

It is certainly not news or an understatement to say that we live in volatile times. Macro- and micro-trends are making life for organizations more difficult and the environment more dynamic. Hypercompetitive markets, geopolitical risk, turbulent commodity prices, the true emergence of the emerging markets, the accelerated ability of technology to quickly create and destroy business models, shorter product life cycles, continuously increasing productivity, and so forth have made managing an organization increasingly challenging. Layer on more specific societal factors and trends—including the continuous increase in online spending, increased access to information via blogs and wikis, democratization of labor across geographies, concerns about wellness and health, the aging of the population in the United States and Europe, the burgeoning youth markets in emerging markets, the calls for alternative energy and green power awareness—and it certainly is a lot for the management of an organization to assimilate. Additionally, in the wake of such fiascos as Enron, WorldCom, Adelphia, Halliburton, and Tyco, there is now increased scrutiny of business performance and methods on the part of government bodies and regulators (e.g., Sarbanes-Oxley, Basel 2) as well as by company boards and activist shareholders.

Given all these factors, how efficiently and dynamically a company manages the allocation of its resources among the possibilities it has before it is the single most important decision a company makes. Every company implicitly allocates its resources and hence has a de facto corporate portfolio even if the company does not view it as such or talk about a portfolio strategy. However, organizations that make a concerted effort to actively manage their corporate portfolios of investments are advantaged in realizing their financial, strategic, and risk objectives and ultimately in creating value. Financial engineering, recruiting the right talent, Six Sigma, and so forth are all important, but they are meaningless if the company is not efficiently generating returns. CPM makes this possible.

At its core, CPM is about empowering a "sharply articulated point of view (POV)" as discussed in Gary Hamel's *Harvard Business Review* (July–August 2000) article on IBM. Hamel states that a powerful POV is credible, coherent, compelling, and commercial. By credible, he implies that the POV must be built upon irrefutable data. Compelling means it must speak to people's emotions, and commercial means it has clear links to the bottom line.[1] CPM is a vehicle and discipline to help you and those in your organization with worthy investment opportunities to sharpen their POV so that those opportunities not worthy of resources can be cut out.

FRAMEWORK FOR CPM SUCCESS

There are two main levers one must influence to enable a CPM capability and ensure that it becomes part of the organization's fiber and not an ephemeral idea; these are process and organizational behavior. Trying to enable CPM without an understanding of the behavioral changes required is foolhardy if not impossible. Because at its core, CPM is a change-management effort that results in competition for resources to optimize a portfolio. And the considerations and organizational requirements involved in optimizing a portfolio at this level are very different from what is required when considering only individual investments or a set of investments within the organization. Most specifically, this means that the leader of one business may have to give up money from one of his or her investments to a peer who has a more attractive investment within that person's business. It may also mean that one product manager within a group has to give up resources to another product manager in the same group. The philosophy behind such a reallocation sounds uncomplicated, but giving up these dollars can have major implications, some tangible and some psychological. By not making a given investment, these leaders may adversely impact the realization of their goals, their span of control, impressions of their business unit's or a product's prospects, and/or internal impressions about their management ability. Given this managerial uncertainty, it is obvious that getting a leader to give up resources for the "greater good," no matter how ideal, is not an easy prospect.

Exhibit 1.1 provides a general framework to use as you embark on bringing CPM to your organization.

The stages of CPM evolution given may not appeal to you in as much as managers never like to think that any part of their organization could be deemed incompetent. But as with any difficult undertaking, a certain amount of unpleasant introspection may be required at an individual or organizational level to know that you could do things better and to admit you have a problem. Only by going through this process have successful organizations realized that there is a better way to do things, ultimately progressing toward what can be described as portfolio management enlightenment. As a result of CPM-enabling efforts, organizations undertaking this are now in better shape, because they are benefiting from the new wisdom and greater understanding that CPM enables. First, let us understand what each of these axes mean and what each stage connotes.

One dimension, *organizational behavior*, is made up of several characteristics, which are listed as follows:

- **Incentive alignment.** What progress has the organization made with reference to the willingness and incentives of its leadership to allocate resources to the best investment opportunities even if they are not their own? To what extent are silos still apparent from a resourcing and decision making perspective? Is taking a balanced view of investment

EXHIBIT 1.1   STAGES OF CPM EVOLUTION

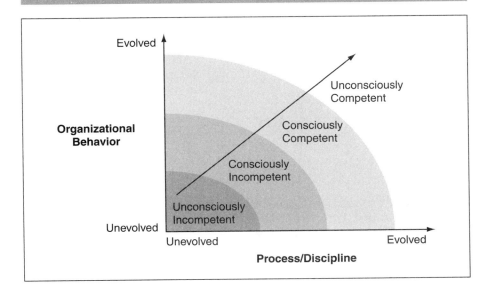

horizons encouraged through proper incentive structures (i.e., are leaders properly considering short- versus long-term investment implications) and are they adequately motivated to pursue long-term, riskier bets? How is accountability built into incentive schemes (i.e., compensation, promotions, and so forth to ensure that leaders ultimately are held responsible for negative performance and rewarded for superior performance)?

- **Cross-functional/organizational cooperation.** When considering an investment, are the various functional areas within an organization working on an investment together? For example, a marketing investment not only captures requisite feedback from marketing but also has inputs from requisite experts in operations, technologies, and finance to come up with a full and robust view of the investment. Silos are not just across business segments within an organization but can be also exhibited cross-functionally in organizations that are not evolved behaviorally.

- **Decision-making style.** Does the organization rely on the gut instinct of its people, whether the intuitive instincts of an elite few or the more general intuitions of a larger segment of the organization's population? To what extent are data-driven, analytical decisions favored? What is the mix of intuitive versus analytical decision making?

The other dimension, *process*, includes the following characteristics:

- **Standardization.** Is the definition of what is an investment clear within the organization and sufficiently comprehensive? Are cost/benefit analyses (CBAs) across the organization standardized when measuring financial, risk, and strategic returns?

- **Robustness.** Are driver-based models used to perform CBAs, and are risks and strategic benefits and concerns sufficiently well-defined and comprehensive?

- **Appropriate centralization.** If there are driver-based models, are global assumptions such as discount rate, foreign exchange rates, tax and interest rates, and so forth centralized across the organization in a way that promotes consistency in investment modeling? Additionally, is there an impartial group that can serve as the nerve center for the company's CPM efforts who will be charged with constantly discussing the organization's portfolio and asking provocative questions of initiative owners? It is worth noting that overcentralization of CPM decisions is a negative characteristic of an organization as this disempowers decision makers within business segments, product groups, functional areas, and so forth from making decisions, because there is now some central "black box" where decisions are made. In short, centralization is a balancing act.

- **Tracking.** Are actual results used to inform specific unit or product-specific investment assumptions on a going-forward basis to ensure they are within previously achieved acceptable ranges of performance? Are actuals captured through tracking systems, and can the organization track promise versus performance in order to promote accountability and actually improve future-year performance using these results?

Before we get into each of the levels of the framework, it is also worth noting that you probably cannot impact both dimensions at the same rate (e.g., moving organizational behavior tends to lag process). So as you work on this, realize that the process is what you will work on first. Why? Because process is something you can directly impact and exert more control over. You can influence standardization, building robust processes and models, appropriate centralization and tracking of investments as long as you are willing to invest time and resources into doing so. Behavior requires changing habits that may have been learned and have become habitual over many years. It may also potentially require changing incentive compensation and promotion structures, which are very difficult to change. Think of the process as a torch that can lead the way for behavioral change once people start to see the benefits of these process improvements.

If we look at Exhibit 1.2 with the curve representing time, this is what organizations can roughly expect as they try to enable CPM.

Now, finally, let us describe what each of the evolution levels implies.

Unconsciously Incompetent

An unconsciously incompetent organization is one that does not know what CPM is or does not care to understand CPM. From a behavioral perspective, the unconsciously incompetent organization is one:

- With silos where individual unit managers or product groups do what is in their best interest with little visibility at an enterprise level as to how these decisions are impacting overall company performance.

EXHIBIT I.2   CPM PROGRESSION OVER TIME

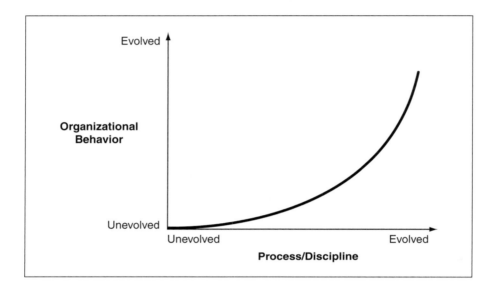

- Where intuitive, decibel-driven decisions are favored over rigorous analytical, data-driven decision making.
- Where incentives do not promote optimal CPM across the enterprise but instead focus on individual unit, product, and market performance. In essence, the organization's current incentives reinforce silos.

From a process perspective, this is typically an organization in which

- There is an unambiguous, at best, definition of what is deemed an investment.
- Modeling of investments is done unsystematically and inconsistently with no driver-based models or underlying assumptions being standardized to any degree.
- The results of investments are not tracked making the accountability that comes with closing the loop (e.g., comparing promise versus performance) impossible.
- Given the lack of cost/benefit analysis, standardization, risk, and strategic relevance, if considered, are very differently handled, making comparison across investments very difficult.

Business as usual (BAU) is how one might characterize this kind of organization; when asked why they do something a certain way, managers typically reply something to the effect of "That is how we've always done it." That is considered a BAU way of doing things. If your organization is really in this category and you are reading this, you are likely an outlying forward-thinker within the organization. Most progressive, forward-thinking organizations generally will not fall into this category as they are always looking for ways to improve their decision making.

Consciously Incompetent

A consciously incompetent organization is one that knows that it could be handling its corporate portfolio better. As mentioned, this is an organization that has admitted it has a problem and that has at least started to try to improve, from a process and behavior perspective. From a process perspective, the consciously incompetent organization

- Has made some strides to standardize the modeling of investments and has also made some efforts to create more rigorous driver-based models.
- Has also probably begun to define specifically what an investment is and has sought to review investments at some aggregated level.
- Still relies on intuitive decision making, predominantly over data-driven, analytical decisions but is making strides on using data-driven analytics to make investment evaluations and conclusions.
- Has established some tracking systems to capture investment performance but still cannot track individual investment results. Forcing accountability at an initiative level is still elusive for a consciously incompetent organization.

The evolution of organizational behavior within consciously incompetent organizations is not very significant and is usually typified by

- Silos and decibel-driven decision making—but attempts are being made to market the idea of CPM among decision makers.
- Incentives not aligned with optimal portfolio management—but there is a realization that incentives and accountability need to be re-aligned in order to enable this.

Most managers reading this book probably fall into this category.

Moving from the consciously incompetent stage to the next level, consciously competent, is likely to be the hardest part of your CPM journey. This complexity is partially because it is easy to regress back to conscious incompetence if you declare victory too early and decide prematurely that your CPM efforts and goals are further along than they actually are. This miscalculation can lull you into a state of complacency, which is dangerous in your pursuit of CPM.

Consciously Competent

A consciously competent organization is one that has steadily worked at CPM; it has adroitly changed organizational behavior to consider CPM when making decisions, and it has also implemented processes that enable the effective management of CPM at an organizational level. Discussions with several organizations revealed how truly difficult it is to move an organization's CPM efforts into the conscious competence category and, in fact, how few organizations even fall into this category.

From a process standpoint, consciously competent organizations

- Are characterized by well-defined processes that provide a concrete and comprehensive definition of what an investment is.
- Have defined methods to model financial returns and have created frameworks that enable comparison of investments across financial, strategic, and risk parameters.
- Possess a healthy mix of analytical and intuition-based decision making to select investments.
- Leverage tracking systems that capture investment actuals to ultimately enable a closed loop against investment projections. As a result of this, the organization is able to force accountability and ultimately to improve future investment performance by leveraging this closed-loop results tracking.

From a behavioral perspective, the consciously competent organization

- Still has managers of different groups vehemently fighting for resources to fund their investments, but there is a corporate and general understanding that managers must fund the initiatives that are best for the entire organization. In fact, the hallmark of a consciously competent organization is that it has succeeded in redeploying money between various groups and investments.

- Has different functional areas partnering to create an investment CBA. This means that groups such as marketing, operations, or finance all talk in a language that relates decisions back to their portfolios.

Unconsciously Competent

An unconsciously competent organization is one where CPM has become part of its DNA and that engages in processes and behaviors that support an optimized corporate portfolio. Unfortunately, there are no examples of unconscious competence I have come across. In all honesty, unconscious incompetence is an aspiration—enlightenment or nirvana for an organization's investment portfolio.

Like a company that seeks to redefine the market segment it is in so that it always has less than 10% market share, companies can never really become unconsciously competent, because they always need to look at their CPM capability and reevaluate and improve upon it. Companies that have even approached unconscious competence are likely to strive for this continuous excellence in their CPM practices and see CPM as a competitive differentiator and advantage that they can always enhance.

What Should Be Considered an Investment?

This is a seemingly innocuous question, but after many discussions with current and aspiring practitioners of CPM, it became apparent that organizations find this a very difficult question to answer. Even after being "answered," it continues to be the source of consistent and ongoing debate within the organization.

Most generally, an investment, from a CPM perspective, should be anything that is discretionary (e.g., it is not required to keep the machine running, the lights on, etc.). Most people agree with this definition on an emotional level, but after a bit more probing, it becomes apparent that many things that are discretionary have managed to creep into the BAU or steady-state buckets.

The trap that it seems most organizations fall into is to spend lots of time discussing and aiming to optimize larger capital expenditures, which they view as discretionary, and little to no time on operating expenses, which many view as required. However, you need not dig far to determine that much of what is in the OpEx line item really is discretionary (e.g., marketing, sales, IT, operations, etc.). Just ask yourself, "Do we really have to invest in the brand advertising campaign?" or "Should we hire five more salespeople?" or "Is that website upgrade absolutely required?" and you will quickly realize that the answer is often that these things are not required and that there is a resource allocation choice to be made here. Companies often think of optimization vertically (e.g., lines of business or products, which role up into business segments, which role up to the enterprise level, as shown in Exhibit 1.3).

However, looking at an organization vertically is not comprehensive enough, because you also need to look at what is discretionary among functional group investments for areas, among others, which are given in Exhibit 1.4.

We will look at applying CPM to each of these areas in more detail later in Chapter 3, Applying CPM to Specific Areas within the Organization, but the main point is that an organization must cast a wide net to capture what is truly discretionary, because letting certain types of discretionary

EXHIBIT 1.3   CPM APPLICABILITY AT VARIOUS ORGANIZATIONAL LEVELS

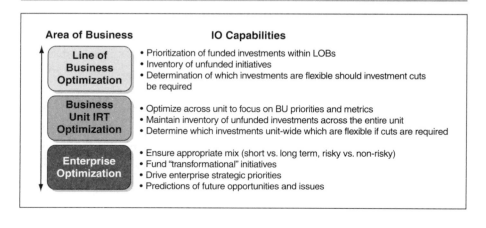

EXHIBIT 1.4   **CPM APPLICABILITY ACROSS FUNCTIONAL AREAS**

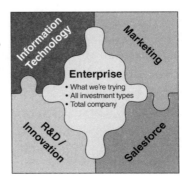

- Where are we investing IT money?
- What value is it bringing to the business?
- How do I communicate this value to my senior management and other stakeholders?

Information Technology

Marketing

- What channels, marketing efforts do we have underway and what is ROI of those efforts?
- What are the best marketing channels, efforts to utilize?

Enterprise
- What we're trying
- All investment types
- Total company

- What does our R&D/Innovation pipeline look like?
- What is our mix of disruptive vs. incremental innovation?
- Are things progressing quick enough?
- What is the viability of R&D/ Innovation efforts?

R&D/ Innovation

Salesforce

- What opportunities does my salesforce have before them?
- Are the opportunities available sufficient in value?
- Are all people on my sales team bringing enough value?

spending slip under the radar will encourage employees to game the system in an effort to circumvent the CPM discipline.

In fact, the average among companies surveyed reveals that 30 to 40% of OpEx truly is discretionary. That is a massive number that currently gets allotted to business leaders as a sort of birthright every year. Whether your organization has $10 million or $1 billion of operating expenses, imagine the impact of taking 30 to 40% of that expense base and optimizing it even marginally and consider its implications on cash flow, operating metrics, and so forth. The potential is incredible.

A word of caution here before the overzealous among you go to parts of your organization and say, "Next year, you are only going to get 60 to 70% of your current year operating expenses, because the rest is discretionary and we'll decide where it should go." This is a quick way to create enemies and sufficiently ensure that CPM goes nowhere fast within your organization. This extreme zero-basing of the portfolio implies every dollar of discretionary investment resources is up for grabs. This is bad for many reasons as you may be able to imagine.

- **It disempowers the subject matter experts.** When you aim to take all the discretionary resources away from group leaders, you are making them impotent. What is their role in growing and building the organization if all the discretionary decisions are taken from them by some central governing body?

- **It results in bad decisions.** More importantly, the decisions that such a central body makes will be suboptimal 90% of the time compared with the subject matter expert's decisions, because this central group does not have the time and experience required to understand the business. This central body's decisions would be made on much more superficial grounds (financial attractiveness, which is perhaps coupled with some consideration of risk and strategy) than the subject matter experts, who generally have a greater understanding of their business's dynamics, their competitors, and other relevant matters.

- **It causes constructive conflict to dissipate.** This type of action by any such central body ultimately results in a view by a segment, functional area, product group, and so forth that this action is some sort of "corporate exercise" or something that "those folks in the Ivory Tower" decided without understanding the business issues, climate, and other important factors. Ultimately, the organization will start to close up and groups will fortify their individual silos. While the idea behind CPM is to enable greater transparency and openness to foster better decisions, this type of action results in the exact opposite. Ultimately, the organization may get the central body's recommendations and take what they like and then take the remainder of their resources and do as they like with it with little to no regard for this central body.

- **It is a waste of time.** People running the business are there for a reason as are people in "corporate," who usually perform a host of analytical, strategic, or process functions. While the two should interact and exchange information and debate ideas, this type of exercise results in all parties not playing to their strengths and ultimately frittering away energy and time.

American Express which is chronicled later in a case study is quite evolved in its use of CPM and has found a good way to keep people engaged with CPM while still not falling into the traps of zero-basing. On a biannual basis, American Express, which has deployed CPM across its entire enterprise, asks the business segment owners to give up the funding associated with their bottom 10% of investments. It enables the segment owners to determine what is the bottom 10% through a mix of any metrics they like. The main result is that the company then puts "up for grabs" a very significant pool of money, which the business segments then compete for. This method is effective because it acknowledges the unit owners' subject matter expertise by letting them retain 90% of their funding. The investment review team (IRT), as it is known at the company, is looking to optimize the portfolio by removing the least attractive investments first. This pragmatic "low-hanging fruit" way of approaching CPM has resulted in behavioral shifts and actual tangible reallocations of tens of millions of dollars across units. Most interestingly, the reallocations have occurred with participation and consent across business segment lines for the first time in the company's history.

MISMANAGING YOUR CORPORATE INVESTMENT PORTFOLIO: THE SEVEN (AND A HALF) DEADLY SINS

The implications of mismanaging a corporate portfolio can be serious. These problems become more acute when you have a competitor or potential new entrant into your arena that is not making the same portfolio management mistakes. The following sections detail the seven (and a half) deadly sins of CPM. Some of these malignant practices have been alluded to earlier, but given their ability to torpedo an organization's corporate portfolio efforts, they are worthy of repetition. After reviewing these sins, do not worry if you find yourself committing one or more of them. Self-awareness is the first step. Once you take action, your organization will be on its way.

Sin 1: Narrowly Defining the Portfolio

A lot of companies focus much of their effort on optimizing their capital expenditures. And because these are often large, multi-year investments with major implications for future company growth, it makes sense that scrutiny is applied to these investments. However, a corporation's focus on CapEx often takes needed attention away from OpEx, which is often assumed to be steady-state or BAU when, in fact, much of it is truly discretionary in nature (e.g., marketing, IT, operations, sales force, etc.). By narrowly defining their view of which investments are worth optimizing, many companies are missing out on a huge opportunity to improve performance and accountability.

Another area in which companies have moved toward a portfolio-management approach is information technology (IT). This appears to be driven mainly by the emergence of the project portfolio management (PPM) vendors, who seem to exclusively target IT, but again, this is a limited way of defining the portfolio, given that IT is only one of the large components of expense at many companies.

If the initial rationalizing of what is a portfolio, is due to a conscious decision to walk before one runs, then this is a prudent and pragmatic approach that makes sense. Show the applicability of CPM within one important arena and then use those results and support to introduce CPM in other parts of the organization. But if your view is that CPM applies only to CapEx or IT or just one particular area, you will not be able to realize the transformational benefits that CPM can afford your organization because of this narrow view.

Sin 2: Investment Decisions Are Like New Year's Resolutions

In their book, *Beyond Budgeting: How Managers Can Break Free from the Annual Performance Trap* (Harvard Business School Press, 2003), Jeremy Hope and Robin Fraser talk about the "annual performance trap" as it relates to budgeting and planning. Unfortunately, the same phenomenon seems to have entrapped many organizations, which view their investment decisions like New Year's resolutions—something you talk about at the beginning of the year but generally forget over time.

This is grossly counter to the way a company's portfolio should be treated. Given the previously mentioned dynamism of the world from both macro and competitive perspectives, this portfolio inertia is very dangerous. How do you respond to competitive threats? How do you know a product is launching when it should or delivering the short-term results that were expected? Where do you invest additional available money due to better than expected performance or some one-time extraordinary event? Viewing your investments and portfolio as a once–a–year event means you are not ready to react to such situations and hence the flexibility, adaptability, and accountability of your organization is minimized.

CPM requires that you are always updating your portfolio of investments with accurate and current information so that you can rebalance your portfolio dynamically over time as needed. It also forces you to determine which investments are flexible so that if negative events occur that require reducing investment spending, these investments can be turned off or scaled back. Negative events can be company specific (e.g., a need to reallocate funding to another market to take advantage of a new opportunity or to fend off a competitor, a need to reduce funding for a marketing campaign in order to redeploy those funds to a compliance/mandatory project). Negative events can also be macro-oriented (e.g., country-specific risks such as political, currency, etc.) which require a rethinking of investments in a particular market. Currency devaluation in several Latin American countries, SARS, the September 2006 coup in Thailand, terrorist actions in London and/or Madrid are all potentially negative events that may change your investment portfolio even on a temporary basis.

Sin 3: Decibel-Driven versus Data-Driven Decision Making

There is an old business adage that says "If it's not being measured, it's not being managed," and with reference to optimizing CPM, there is definitely not a more appropriate comment. CPM is about data-driven, objectives-based decisions. It is about removing the decibels from decision making (i.e., the non-objective, personality-driven reasons projects happen). This does not mean that every investment will have a rigorous cost/benefit analysis underlying it as it is difficult if not impossible to always quantify the impact of an investment, but the majority of investments should have measurable and defined metrics or milestones associated with them. But many times this type of metric- or milestone-based accountability is hindered by several types of characters (people or groups) who drive decibel-driven decisions. Some of the main proponents/characters of decibel-driven decisions are:

- **The closer.** This is the charismatic salesperson within an organization who through a combination of charisma, relationship management, and pretty PowerPoint presentations receives funding for projects without a solid underlying business case, metrics, milestones, and so on. This is likely a person who has significant credibility within the organization based on past performance and, therefore, can leverage those results to generate ongoing belief in his or her business acumen. Irrespective of your past successes, a good CPM process will require rigor in all investments being evaluated.

- **The screamer.** This is the person (or group) who most forcefully declares the need for funding—the person who literally drives decibel-driven decisions.

- **The end-arounder.** This is the person (or group) who will get a request for funding denied by the people facilitating CPM but will then approach the CFO, CEO, or CIO directly and use those relationships with senior decision makers to make a case and receive funding.

- **The strategist.** Strategy is important and, as discussed, it is inherently tied to portfolio management, but many times, strategy is the rationale for an investment that you cannot convey the benefit of. *Q:* "Why do we need to make this investment where there are no return data?" *A:* "For strategic reasons." Undoubtedly, there will be instances where an investment cannot be quantified, and so one's business instinct and strategic considerations need to be relied upon, but be careful of having too many investments fall into the "it's strategic" category. This is a catch-all for people who have difficulty conveying the benefit of their investments.

- **The doomsdayer.** Doomsdayers do not have rigorous milestones or metrics associated with their investment but instead rely on fear as a justification for their investments. One example within many organizations is in IT investments around security (i.e., "If we don't do this $10 million investment, our customer data may become available or vulnerable"). It is also a favorite when looking at competitive threats (e.g., "Although the economics of this product make it a loss-leader, not launching such a product will cause us to lose market share to our competitor."). These fear-based rationales can have some validity, but the thesis supporting an investment should not be solely fear based.

- **The optimist.** This is the person who has not grasped the idea of sunk costs and is consistently guilty of taking ill-advised projects entirely too far. Some projects are "doomed to completion" as the CFO Executive Board has explained, and the optimist is guilty of running these projects. The optimist will contend, "We've already invested so much in this project over the last two years, and although late, we are only one year away from realizing the benefits." Past investment of money, effort, and resources are not a reason to complete a project, no matter how positive the project sponsor is of the project's benefits. Organizations must take a long, hard look at such projects and determine if the benefits and risks are still reasonable and worth bearing as well as deciding on the merits of these updated expectations. Using resources for such projects saddles the organization's portfolio with losers that take resources away from better initiatives. Opportunity cost and opportunities lost are important to consider when funding the initiatives of an optimist.

Even with this colorful cast of characters promoting decibel-driven decisions, it is important that subjective, intuitive elements of investment selection not be omitted, but just balanced. Generally, organizations heavily rely on instinct and intuition, but an organization looking to improve portfolio performance must embrace a data-driven culture to bring balance to the analytical versus intuitive decision-making process. The motivation for doing this is simple—data-driven decisions work.

To demonstrate that data works, there are numerous examples where data has prevailed over conventional, intuitive, decibel-led decision making. Following are three diverse and somewhat surprising applications of data that show how decision-making capabilities are improved.

Example One: Improving the ability of a doctor to determine whether a patient is having a heart attack   The following example is detailed excellently in Malcolm Gladwell's book, *Blink*,[2] and is summarized as a great example of the power of data. In 1996, Dr. Brendan Reilly became the chairman of Cook County Hospital's Department of Medicine. The hospital was in disarray with inadequate funding and facilities and was overwhelmed by patient inflow as it was the "place of last resort for the hundreds of thousands of Chicagoans without health insurance."[3] In his efforts to improve Cook County, Dr. Reilly changed the method its doctors used to diagnose patients coming to the emergency room complaining of chest pain. On average, 30 people came into Cook County Hospital per day complaining they were having a heart attack. And since these 30 used an inordinate share of resources (e.g., beds, doctor and nurse time, etc.) and stayed around for longer than other patients, it was important to ensure that these patients were treated appropriately but also expeditiously, especially in cases where they were not having a heart attack. But this was not the case. "Chest-pain patients were resource intensive. The treatment protocol was long and elaborate and—worst of all—maddeningly inconclusive."[4]

To prove this, Reilly conducted a bit of an experiment. He "put together twenty perfectly typical case histories of people with chest pain and gave the histories to a group of doctors—cardiologists, internists, emergency room docs, and medical residents—people, in other words, who had lots of experience making estimates about chest pain. The point was to see how much agreement there was about who among the twenty cases was actually having a heart attack. What Reilly found was that there really wasn't any agreement at all. The answers were all over the map. The same patient might be sent home by one doctor and checked into intensive care by another." Although doctors and staff would try to make reasoned, evidence-led decisions, Reilly determined that their decisions appeared to be more like guesses than based on well-constructed logic. "We asked the doctor to estimate on a scale of zero to one hundred the probability that each patient was having an acute myocardial infarction [heart attack] and the odds that each patient would have a major life-threatening complication in the next three days. In each case, the answers we got pretty much ranged from zero to one hundred. It was extraordinary, "Reilly commented.[5]

And since between 2 to 8% of the time in U.S. hospitals a patient gets sent home who is truly having a heart attack, doctors err on the side of caution by collecting all of the information they can. But, as mentioned, the caution exhibited by Cook County Hospital doctors led to the hospital's resources being utilized on patients who might not actually be having heart attacks and hence could be sent home.

How did Dr. Reilly tackle the inconclusiveness of the doctor findings and develop a more rational approach to making heart attack diagnoses? Reilly turned to the work of a cardiologist, Lee Goldman, and a group of mathematicians who compiled hundreds of heart attack cases and evaluated them from a mathematical perspective. And he took this formerly highly qualitative and subjective analysis and synthesized it into an algorithm that he felt would remove much of the indecision and inconclusiveness of the process. "Doctors," he concluded, "ought to combine the evidence of the ECG with three of what he called urgent risk factors: (1) Is the pain felt by the patient unstable angina? (2) Is there fluid in the patient's lungs? and (3) Is the patient's systolic blood pressure below 100?"

"For each combination of risk factors, Goldman drew up a decision tree that recommended a treatment option." Reilly embraced Goldman's approach and conducted a "bake-off" at Cook County. "For the first few months, the staff would use their own judgment in evaluating chest pain. . . . Then they would use Goldman's algorithm, and the diagnosis and outcome of every patient treated under the two systems would be compared. For two years, data were collected, and in the end, the result wasn't even close. Goldman's rule won hands down in two directions: it was a whopping 70 percent better than the old method at recognizing the patients who weren't actually having a heart attack. At the same time, it was safer . . . . Left to their own devices, the doctors guessed right on the most serious patients somewhere between 75 and 89 percent of the time. The algorithm guessed right more than 95 percent of the time." Data wins.

Example Two: Picking Oscar-winning films without reading scripts
JP Morgan's John Miller has financed many recent Oscar-winning movies including *Million Dollar Baby*, *Gladiator*, and *American Beauty*, to name a few. Largely, because of his movie-picking prowess, JP Morgan is the dominant player in the movie financing business with 80% of the market. Miller's ability has given JP Morgan a competitive advantage that has led to share gain, but it has also led to the bank's being able to charge a premium over others. Miller is able "to charge interest rates of up to three percentage points over the rate that top banks pay to borrow from each other. That's on top of fees of up to 3% of the loan commitment. It makes for a lucrative profit center: Miller says margins for the business can reach 80% of revenues."[6]

So has JP Morgan found a movie aficionado with an uncanny, intuitive eagle's eye for picking winning movies? Actually, the bank found the exact opposite. As *BusinessWeek* reported on Miller, "He's strictly a numbers guy. Although he often goes to the movies, he doesn't read scripts, doesn't care about plots, and doesn't worry about which stars have signed on—unless they threaten to bust the budget. He relies instead on a sophisticated financing model fueled by data on how more than 300 films performed at the box office. It allows him to tune out the noise and focus on what really counts in a movie's success: its business plan, especially its budget, release date, genre, and distribution schedule."

If Miller can utilize data to make decisions in what is arguably one of the most haphazard and historically gut-instinct businesses in the world, data-driven decisions are validated once again.

Example Three: Managing the evaluation and selection of baseball players for the major leagues   In Michael Lewis's book *Moneyball: The Art of Winning an Unfair Game*,[7] Lewis explores how the general manager of the Oakland Athletics utilizes an atypical yet highly effective new approach to running his team in order to produce outstanding results.

The central premise of *Moneyball* is that the collected wisdom of baseball insiders (including players, managers, coaches, scouts, and the front office) over the past century is subjective and often flawed. Statistics such as 40-yard dash times, RBIs, and batting average, typically used to gauge players, are relics of a 19th-century view of the game and the statistics that were available at the time.

Since then, real statistical analysis has shown that on-base percentage and slugging percentage are better indicators of offensive success and that avoiding an out is more important than getting a hit. This flies in the face of conventional baseball wisdom and the beliefs of many of the men who are paid large sums to evaluate talent.

By reevaluating the strategies that produce wins on the field, the Athletics, with approximately $55 million in salary, are competitive with the New York Yankees who spend over $205 million (in 2005–06) annually on their players. Oakland is forced to find players undervalued by the market, and their system for finding value in undervalued players has proven itself thus far.

Baseball traditionalists, in particular some scouts and media members, decry the sabermetric revolution and have disparaged *Moneyball* for going against traditional thinking. Nevertheless, the impact of *Moneyball* upon major league front offices is undeniable. In its wake, teams such as the New York Mets, New York Yankees, San Diego Padres, St. Louis Cardinals, Washington Nationals, Arizona Diamondbacks, and the Toronto Blue Jays have hired full-time statistical analysts."[8]

The *Moneyball* example is among the richest examples of data-driven decisions as it underscores several important themes. Most obviously, the ability of Billy Beane (general manager of the Oakland Athletics) to look past conventional, go-with-our-gut instinctive decisions to player choices based on data-driven analysis is a great lesson in the power of analytical decision making. Just as important, Beane's ability to do this shows how organizations with significantly less in the way of resources (the Athletics in this example) can compete with the big boys within their industry (e.g., the New York Yankees). From an upstart or emerging company perspective, the Athletics demonstrated that resource optimization can and will level the playing field with much larger, more resourced competitors. If every dollar you spend is more efficient (i.e., produces greater returns—in a quantitative and qualitative sense) than your larger rivals, you will close the gap over time. For larger, established companies, this is an opportunity and warning. If you can optimize your resource allocation, you can catch up with or extend your lead on players of all sizes—large and small. If, however, your resource utilization is not efficient, you will be eclipsed by a competitor. The question is when, not if. Unfortunately, your organization will probably not have as easy a management scorecard as a baseball team—wins and losses. As a result, the need for CPM becomes even more acute.

Sin 4: Too Many Metrics, Not Enough Time

So data-driven, analytical decisions are essential for CPM, but can you have too much of a good thing? While the data drivers and metrics associated with an investment can help guide your business, an organization must be careful not to "boil the ocean" when it comes to determining which pieces of data are important and which are not. The main problem with too many metrics is that although most do not have significant impact on investment performance or how to manage the company, they take significant time to create, compile, and analyze. But by having a long list of drivers and metrics, companies often are lulled into a sense of accomplishment. "We have a management dashboard which tracks the 73 most important drivers of our business." This is not good management. It is confusion. So, one of the primary objectives your organization should have is determining which investment drivers and result metrics really impact how you run your business and how your business performs.

Hopefully, these drivers and metrics map well against one another. Performing sensitivity or other statistical analyses of your various drivers can help you distill down what really impacts the CBAs you put together in your organization. By determining the appropriate drivers, you can also ensure that people within the organization are using acceptable assumptions when building business cases. By refining the output metrics that are going to be looked at, you can help guide investment owners to focus on what is important and increase accountability for actual results that matter. If you have 50 different output metrics you determine to be important, the message to people putting forward investment proposals is ambiguous. An example of where the wrong metrics are being looked at can be seen in the current craze for innovation. The metrics companies look at to determine their progress against innovation include number of patents filed or number of opportunities reviewed and killed or dollars spent on innovative projects. Do these metrics really tell you how innovative your company is? Does the number of patents just incentivize people to patent everything and anything? Does looking at number of opportunities killed give you any insights into the quality of the ideas that have come into the process? Does the amount of dollars invested in innovative projects tell you whether those ideas are good ones, whether the projects are progressing as they should, or, more fundamentally, does it tell you if people within the organization are defining innovation in the same way?

As Gladwell stated in *Blink*, it is important for the sake of expediency and good decision making to use what psychologists refer to as the "power of thin-slicing," which says that as human beings we are capable of making sense of situations based on the thinnest slice of experience. Data is required, but an over-reliance on it will slow you down and ultimately cause bad decisions or, even worse, indecision. Your intuitive ability to thin-slice is necessary and valuable when used appropriately. When used in conjunction with analytics, it makes for a very powerful symbiotic relationship.

Sin 5: One-Size-Fits-All Portfolio Management

Often, companies undertaking the deployment of CPM aim to optimize a metric or use a framework to determine how they should be allocating their resources. In short, if a single framework or metric could help you determine how to make resource allocation decisions, your individual talents would not be needed. Let us take a look at an example of a fictitious metrics-oriented organization, MetricsCo, Inc. MetricsCo initially determined that return on investment (ROI) would be the main metric it would choose to optimize and that it would fund only investments with an ROI of over 100%. In essence, all MetricsCo has to do to pick where to allocate resource is to compile a list of its investments, sort it in Excel by ROI, draw a line at 100%, and action the investments that have an ROI of over 100%. Quite simple, right? Yes indeed, and wholly inadequate and ineffective. Doing this does not consider risk, strategy, the validity of assumptions driving these investments, or the most basic idea of a portfolio that says that you probably want to have a mix of investment types (i.e., those that are low risk where you are fairly certain of your returns coupled with those that are more innovative or riskier where the results are more uncertain but that you want to do in order to enable organizational growth).

Let us assume MetricsCo realizes the inadequacy of its ROI-oriented portfolio and moves to an investment-scoring methodology according to which it will consider various return characteristics to give each investment a score that can be used to compare across investments. With its new, more "rigorous" evaluation technique, MetricsCo weighs ROI 33%, net present value (NPV) 33%, and five-year revenue growth 33% to develop this investment score. Again, this technique, while a modest improvement over using just ROI, fails to consider risk, strategy, the validity of assumptions driving these metrics, and investment mix.

After realizing the fallacy of this investment scoring method of picking investments, MetricsCo decides to develop a more rigorous resource allocation framework that considers risk and returns. The company determines that payback period is the risk metric and ROI is the return metric to look at in its resource allocation framework and puts together the following 2×2 (see Exhibit 1.5) on which they plot their investments.

This framework would then "tell the organization" to fund those investments that are in quadrant 4 (i.e., high ROI, short payback period). Again, the same issues arise. While this may be a useful diagnostic to determine whether the company should be doing more or less of certain types of investments or to spur questions about certain investments, organizations must prevent the urge to use their CPM process as a "black box" to make investment decisions.

The impression on the behalf of initiative owners that CPM is a means for some central body to make decisions for their area and the organization overall can lead to needless conflict within the organization. Moreover, it is unrealistic to expect a central body to make decisions for the entire company based on a framework. A central body reviewing investments across an organization should be able to raise provocative ideas and questions about

EXHIBIT 1.5   METRICSCO SAMPLE RESOURCE
ALLOCATION FRAMEWORK

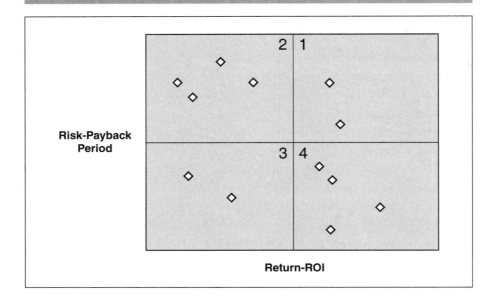

portfolio investments and force transparency and accountability, but it cannot be solely charged with optimizing the portfolio.

Sin 6: If We Install This Software, We Will Be Able to Optimize Our Corporate Portfolio

A whole host of vendors may try to sell you on the proposition that a software solution is required for a CPM discipline. Technology exists that can help with the aggregation, reporting of, and analytics of your organization's portfolio, but there is no technology tool that will optimize your organization's portfolio for you. Many of the currently available tools lack the ability to actually model your investments; instead, they capture data on investments with no ability to determine whether these inputs are realistic or valid with historical performance. Simplistically viewed, this means that initiative owners can type in their investment details and come up with the result that its ROI is 10,000% with some rudimentary checks at best. A driver-based approach would help mitigate some of these issues, but not all.

While many vendors do clearly articulate the benefits of portfolio management, their software's value proposition in realizing these benefits is conceptual at best, although they will point you to results that their tools have delivered. In this case, correlation does not imply causation (i.e., the results delivered are more a function of a committed organization that happened to have a tool versus a tool that has really driven these benefits). Gartner analyst, Matt Light, probably has most eloquently stated the over-emphasis on a technology tool as a solution with his comment at the Gartner Symposium/ITxpo 2006, "A fool with a tool is still a fool." Some industry studies have actually found that 80% of the functionality available in off-the-shelf portfolio management tools is utilized by only 20% of customers. So the question is why invest time, significant money, and resources on a large-scale enterprise deployment of a tool when much of it will not even be utilized? Technology, thoughtfully applied, can help you enable the process with greater efficiency, accountability, and transparency, but it is not the solution or even one of the most essential components of the solution. In fact, adopting a technology tool after you have built a CPM capability and worked through some of the cultural and behavioral elements is beneficial in that you actually have some experience with CPM and can now better articulate to a technology provider what issues you need to solve for or what functionality you would like in the tool. As a result, adopting a technology tool at the outset of implementing a CPM discipline is not advisable.

Sin 7: It Is All about the Projections

If your plan to deploy a CPM discipline across your organization does not include a means to capture actual investment returns, its value is significantly minimized. The ability to compare promise (projections) versus performance (actuals) is a basic underpinning of successful CPM in that it enables accountability within the organization and helps future performance by improving and constantly refining drivers and assumptions used in investment projection creation.

That said, this "closing of the loop" is the single hardest part of CPM. Many organizations do not even have tracking systems or the infrastructure and instead rely on ad hoc methods to track in Excel or access databases, if at all. Many organizations may capture actuals, but they are contained within unwieldly legacy systems. Often enough, those actuals are captured at a more aggregated or disaggregated level than at which an investment projection is created, so truly comparing promise versus performance at an investment level becomes difficult. But this is not required. Even capturing actuals at some aggregated level so that many investments can be aggregated and compared for promise versus performance is of immense value.

As you embark on your path to enabling CPM, keep the closing of the loop in mind as an objective as it is the only way to turn data about investments into knowledge over time.

Sin 7.5: Portfolio Management Is a Tunnel—Not a Funnel

If every project submitted gets reviewed and ultimately funded, an organization's CPM process is not an investment decision-making discipline; rather, it is a bureaucratic exercise that adds little to no value. CPM processes require constructive conflict and discussion and ultimately require that some projects get killed. The funnel analogy means that if 100 investment proposals are submitted, only 75 get funding, for example. This ability to stop projects when proposed or sometime during their delivery if they are not achieving expectations is a key element of keeping your CPM discipline relevant and part of the organization's DNA. It is not the number of projects accepted or killed that is important; people must know that managing the corporate portfolio is serious business, and rejecting bad business cases or ideas is a surefire way to let people know that the organization is serious about funding investments on a meritocratic basis.

Notes

1. Gary Hamel, "Waking up IBM: how a gang of unlikely rebels transformed Big Blue," *Harvard Business Review*, July–August 2000.
2. Little, Brown and Company, 2005.
3. *Blink* by Malcolm Gladwell, p 126.
4. *Ibid*, p 128.
5. *Ibid*, p 130.
6. *BusinessWeek*, March 7, 2005.
7. W.W. Norton, 2003.
8. Wikipedia, http://en.wikipedia.org/wiki/Moneyball

CHAPTER 2

Bringing CPM to Your Organization

In order to deploy corporate portfolio management (CPM) within your organization, you must approach it as an investment that requires resources. CPM does not happen overnight and cannot be the job of one individual within an organization. As with any ambitious cross-organizational effort, the timeline for making CPM a reality can be protracted and the effort can be backbreaking. To keep the momentum for the effort going within the organization and to constantly reinvigorate yourself personally about CPM, you must aim to show results over time. And you must also keep in mind that to really impact and optimize one's corporate portfolio, you need to look at results on a timeframe that is in months and years not days or weeks. CPM is a major change-management exercise. That does not mean that you have to invest in a CPM discipline and just cross your fingers and wait for results to come in. There are interim measures and milestones that should be reached that will give you insights into the efficacy of your CPM efforts.

To this end, a robust game plan is required pre- and post-CPM implementation consisting of four distinct phases (see Exhibit 2.1):

- Analyze
- Galvanize
- Standardize
- Optimize

EXHIBIT 2.1   FOUR PHASES OF CPM IMPLEMENTATION

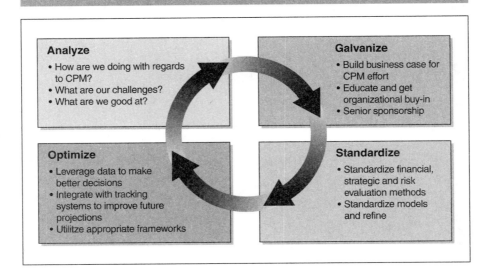

FOUR-STEP ROADMAP TO CPM SUCCESS

Step 1: Analyze

Presumably, you probably already have a hypothesis about how CPM could benefit your company or organization since you have picked up this book. To understand how you are doing today and to build the case for why your organization should undertake CPM, you need to understand your organization's current capabilities, competencies, and assets as well as the organization's aspirations. It also requires taking a hard look at your organization's attitudes, readiness, development areas, and weaknesses to make a pragmatic decision on whether you are ready for CPM and to what extent. And finally, it is always important to understand your personal motivations for wanting to bring CPM to your organization.

The previously discussed organizational behavior versus process/discipline framework is one that can be used for this analysis. It will be augmented with information about your own and your organization's attitude and readiness with regard to CPM. There is a questionnaire (see Exhibit 2.2) to be used in guiding your analysis. You will notice that the analyze phase does not get into quantifying the benefits of CPM as that happens once you have determined that CPM is something you want to do and have moved to the galvanize phase.

Several questions need to be asked to analyze where your organization is today:

Process and Discipline

- How do you currently manage your company's investments?
- Is there an organizational nerve center that people who may be competing for resources will believe? If this group came out with cross-organizational recommendations related to the portfolio, would they be viewed as unbiased and credible?
- What is the evolution of investment tracking within the organization?
- What is deemed an investment within your organization?
- Is there a rigorously created and followed formal organizational strategic plan that serves as the basis for people's actions, goals, and motivations?
- Is there a utilized framework in place to evaluate the risk associated with investments?
- Do you employ a small number of core metrics that are tied to/drive the company's strategic plan? Are the metrics widely accepted across the organization?

Organizational Behavior

- What is the "personality" of your organization and how will CPM fit with this personality?
- What is the "political landscape" of your organization?
- How much time do you have to develop CPM within the organization (i.e., what is your organization's patience level)?
- Is cross-organizational and cross-functional sharing of information occurring and encouraged?
- Are incentives (compensation, promotion, etc.) aligned and configured in a way that promotes total organizational success over individual (i.e., unit, product, and geographic) success? And do incentives consider short- and long-term organizational aspirations?

Attitude and Readiness

- How much would CPM (if done right) help your organization or your company?

- How big of an undertaking is CPM in your estimation within your organization?

- Do you have a senior-level CPM champion within the organization?

- Are there any potential quick but material wins for CPM (i.e., are there specific areas of the company that CPM can be developed in to provide you and the effort with appropriate credibility and momentum)?

- What resources (people or money) will you have at your disposal to deploy and make CPM a reality?

- If CPM is something you are advocating and that you hope to spearhead, what are your personal ambitions and hopes as they relate to CPM?

The questionnaire (Exhibit 2.2) provides a diagnostic that can be used to determine your organization's current competencies and challenges in relation to implementing CPM. Additional information follows that relates to each question; it can be skipped if you have a good understanding of what is being asked and why it is important as you evaluate a CPM approach.

Process and Discipline

Question 1: How do you currently manage your company's discretionary investments?

Considerations: CPM is about improving discretionary investment decision making, and in order to do that, understanding how your organization currently deals with these investments is important. There are several components to this:

- **Rigor.** As previously discussed, rigorous driver-based investment models are preferable as you consider CPM. Since CPM ultimately requires making trade-offs between investments, the use of driver-based models offers a level of thoroughness that will make cross-investment comparison easier and more credible. It also facilitates ongoing improvement of these driver-based models over time using actual performance. As a result, this allows an organization to make better investment projections going forward. Of course, this assumes that these driver-based models were properly created. If you have driver-based models that you do not think are worthwhile or that people within your organization do not buy into, these should not be considered valuable assets along your CPM journey and should be transformed as required.

Also, it is worth understanding whether your organization aspires and has the temperament to migrate toward driver-based models. Some organizations feel that their investments are so diverse that driver-based models are not useful. Others may view driver-based models as a waste of effort because they do not adequately allow for the intuition required in considering an investment. If these comments describe your organization, the move to driver-based models may be obscured, and this can be problematic inasmuch as a high-quality CPM capability requires data to underlie it and form the basis for its portfolio recommendations and optimization.

- **Standardization.** Similar to rigor, standardization of investment models enables comparability across the investments that are at the heart of CPM. When model consistency does not exist, and comparison of investments is attempted, variations in model construction drive differences in investment projections. which will not be accurate. As a result, making constructive analytical and trade-off recommendations regarding these investments becomes impractical. Even if different models yield good data that indicate a particular investment decision, it is possible to obfuscate these recommendations when the models used are dissimilar. Standardization helps keep the focus on the investment results and remove suspicion from the process. This ultimately enables more useful discussions to take place about the corporate portfolio.

  A fundamental precept of CPM is standardization, as it ultimately enables the conversation to stay focused on investment behaviors and allows the dialog to move away from debates about methodology. An organization's ability to move toward a more standardized investment-modeling methodology is central to a successful CPM discipline.

- **Data availability.** Facilitating investment portfolio reviews and reallocations requires that there be an aggregated view of investments across the organization. If data is presently not available for this purpose, it is not a fatal flaw as you embark on your CPM discipline; ultimately, however, a method to collect and aggregate investment data is required to provide a view into the corporate portfolio.

- **Centralization of assumptions.** This dimension is a subset of rigor and standardization. Centralization of assumptions ensures that certain organizationwide assumptions are controlled to allow for better investment projections. Assumptions such as cost of equity, foreign exchange, and tax rates can be controlled centrally to reduce process-driven variability in investment performance. Again, the aim is to remove noise from investment projections and ensure that the focus of investment reviews is on the projections and not the process.

Question 2: Is there an organizational nerve center that people who may be competing for resources will believe? If this central group delivered organizational recommendations regarding the portfolio, would they be viewed as unbiased and credible?

Considerations: Having a group that can serve as the information hub and the credible owners of CPM is important to its long-term success. Understanding whether there is currently a group that can serve as this central body is important because it is this group that will drive the discipline forward and can also serve as the band of people that handles portfolio analysis and the making of recommendations to reallocate resources. For example, the group can be a central finance group, an organization strategic planning group, or even a highly skilled project management office. Group members must possess certain core competencies and attributes in order to serve as steward of the CPM discipline. Their qualifications include

- Being unbiased
- Understanding financial, strategy, and risk elements related to investments to be able to deliver well-constructed portfolio and investment analysis and recommendations
- Possessing organizational credibility so that people will view and accept their recommendations

This is important, because putting CPM in the hands of an upstart group that lacks credibility or burying it in an existing area without these attributes creates a high hurdle from the start. People naturally extrapolate the importance of CPM from the organization heading up the effort—the less important the group heading it up, the less important the initiative. Many organizations make this mistake. For example, they put CPM in the hands of a project management office that may have skills in managing project milestones and work plans but possesses no sense for financial, strategy, and risk analysis. These groups may have the best of intentions, but in the case of CPM, persistence does not always overcome resistance. Giving responsibility for CPM to a group ill-suited for it is a quick way to spend lots of time and money for uncertain returns. Ultimately, CPM is the casualty of this structure. It gets written off as a discipline that does not work, when it was the inappropriate selection of a group to manage the CPM effort that doomed it to failure.

There may be groups that have the right skill set in terms of understanding financial, strategy, and risk, but lack the ability to be unbiased; consequently, there will always be real or expected self-selection in any investment allocations they suggest. Again, such discussions distract from the goals of CPM and focus too much time and energy on process and not enough on really impacting the corporate portfolio.

Where does CPM belong within the organization?

In conversations with companies who have developed or begun to develop inspired CPM capabilities, the nerve center has typically been a central finance organization. The right finance organization obviously understands finance, knows how to review cost/benefit analyses, can help standardize models and assumptions, and generally understands risk; finance groups are usually intrinsically focused on getting the organization to spend more efficiently. Most importantly, the finance function has a hand in setting budgets and expectations of units, product groups, and so forth, and the money that flows through an organization is almost invariably always touched by finance in some way. As a result, finance's control of the purse strings makes it a good fit for managing a CPM effort. Additionally, a central or corporate finance group can also be an unbiased arbiter when trade-off investment decisions need to be made among groups. Finance groups can also play the role of devil's advocate in challenging investment assumptions and initiative owners. Of course, any organization managing the CPM effort must be careful not to play devil's advocate too much, or else their constant questioning will slow down efforts and create antagonism. It is important that any group managing the CPM effort be solutions oriented and not just issues oriented. All of the foregoing discussion regarding finance as the home for CPM assumes that it is the "right" finance organization. If the organization cannot handle basic blocking and tackling finance functions such as budgeting, planning, forecasting, and reporting, it will not have the bandwidth or internal credibility to manage CPM. Often, this credibility is a function of the CFO and the CFO's standing within the organization.

Although finance can be a good envoy for a CPM capability, many organizations have established information technology (IT) PMOs to manage their CPM efforts (at least as it relates to IT investments). "PMO" stands for different things across organizations (e.g., project management office, program management office, or portfolio management office). The naming confusion is a precursor to a more material issue for PMOs—they generally do not work. A *ComputerWorld* article found that two of three PMOs do not succeed in achieving their objectives. While many readers will invariably assume that they belong to that one of three, this is a dangerous assumption- one that is obviously overoptimistic. While conferences about setting up and managing effective IT PMOs continue to make their planners a nice profit, most organizations ultimately gain little real benefit from IT PMOs. So although they have become fashionable, think hard about having an existing or newly established IT PMO manage your CPM effort. PMOs fail for many reasons, including the following:

- **They do not control the purse strings.** PMOs generally do not control the flow of money, making management of a CPM effort difficult.

- **They have the wrong talent.** A successful CPM capability requires people who understand finance, strategy, and risk, and IT PMOs are generally staffed with technologists who, more often than not, do not possess the requisite skills to adequately understand the parameters required for CPM.

- **They focus on the wrong things.** IT PMOs worry about projects that blow budgets or those that fall behind schedules or that fail to deliver what they said they would. However, the question of whether the investment was worth doing from the start is rarely considered. Yes, there are reams of questionnaires and information that have to be submitted to start the project, but these are typically not used to understand the appropriateness of the projects being considered.

- **They are impotent devil's advocates.** Related to the purse strings issue, IT PMOs generally have a dubious reputation. They do not control the flow of money; instead, they harass their IT colleagues by finding mistakes and issues with what is submitted and reporting that back to management. As a result, IT initiative owners are motivated to circumvent the IT PMO processes when possible. If the PMOs had control of funding (generally in the hands of business partners), they would have some leverage in the CPM picture.

- **They overestimate the power of technology.** Many IT PMOs are enamored with the idea of a tool for managing their PMO efforts and realizing their objectives. Again, customizing a tool provides countless hours of activity, but unless there is a solid process underlying that tool, the tool is enabling vapor. Activity does not equate to progress.

Many who are in or managing PMOs will vehemently disagree about the effectiveness of IT PMOs, but if your organization exhibits any of the aforementioned characteristics, you may be in the 66% (or I suspect more that fail). PMOs can be valuable, however, and their functional expertise about the health and viability of a technologies project can be combined with an appropriate finance or strategic planning group to evaluate larger investments on an initial and ongoing basis. They can also be actively engaged in IT stage gating processes in partnership with finance or strategy groups.

Question 3: What is the evolution of investment tracking within the organization?

Considerations: Truly evolved CPM requires that a virtuous feedback loop be created that feeds future-year investment projections based on past-year investment results. In organizations of any complexity, this is often difficult as the systems that contain tracking information either do not exist or the tracking information is available only at an aggregate level, making comparison of projections and performance nearly impossible. Understanding your company's current tracking capabilities, their willingness to invest more in this area if needed, and the overall complexity of tracking infrastructure is important. If data is available but spread across many different platforms, this creates more complexity for an organization as it attempts to close the loop on investments.

Question 4: What is deemed an investment within your organization?

Considerations: How restrained is your organization's view of investments? Is it only the largest capital expenditures, or are many things considered discretionary including aspects of operating expenses? The current definition of investments tells an organization where CPM can be deployed today and serves as a filter to determine whether CPM is really requisite. If your definition of investments yields three large capital expenditures, the rigor and other aspects of CPM may be requisite, but then again, they may be overkill. However, if your current investment definition is restrained, with the intention of expanding it in the future, CPM may be useful in this regard. Organizations that are willing to put more into the discretionary pool are also signaling that there are no "sacred cows" when it comes to investments and are therefore indicating their commitment to CPM.

A more insidious organizational issue arises when firms do not have a definition for what is and what is not an investment. This is surprising on the surface but a very major reality, given that many organizations have developed budgets and budgeting processes in which the discretionary projects that make up a portion of the budget are deemed as business as usual and not really as discretionary. If your organization does not have a definition of investment, you face a paradox of sorts. Yours is an organization that probably would benefit significantly from a CPM discipline, but given its lack of an investment definition, your organization would probably also require significant exertion to make CPM successful.

Question 5: Is there a rigorously created and followed formal organizational strategic plan that serves as the basis for people's actions, goals, and priorities?

Considerations: CPM is an effort to optimize resource allocation and resource allocation is strategy (i.e., where you allocate your resources is your strategy). Having an organizational strategic plan can serve as a foundation for CPM work inasmuch as the portfolio analytics and recommendations can always be tied back to the strategic plan to ensure adherence to the company's stated strategy. If a strategic plan is not in place, CPM is still possible, but the recommendations it may reveal cannot be grounded using the strategic plan as a framework, and this can lead to some inefficiencies in the process. That said, the lack of a strategic plan may be a positive in some ways, because it causes more dialog about investments and what the organization should be doing. Consequently, it can actually lead to a de facto strategic plan based on the resource allocation that occurs. However, this is a bit like the tail wagging the dog; a strategic plan ideally should shape the portfolio. The CPM effort, if utilized on an ongoing basis, should help to refine the strategic plan based on risks being seen and on the returns that are being achieved.

Question 6: Is there a utilized framework in place to evaluate the risk associated with investments?

Considerations: As you consider investments and making investment trade-offs, thinking past cost/benefit analyses and strategy is important, because risk needs to be figured in to investment evaluation as well. Having a rigorous and standardized framework that considers operational, credit, and market risk with regard to individual investments is required to fully evaluate and ultimately develop a full view of investments—that is, the reward (financial and strategic return) with risk. Often, the development of an organizational risk framework can be complex and challenging to syndicate, given people's different perspectives on what should be evaluated in risk. But developing a good standard structure for risk assessment allows you to evaluate investments on a like versus like basis. A risk framework is not a black box that can be relied on as the end-all for risk evaluation, but it should provide a good starting point for conversation.

The conversation that is possible once you have a solid risk framework in place can really help to optimize a corporate portfolio. With good investment information about risk, financial, and strategic benefits, you have the requisite levers to make trade-off decisions and balance your portfolio adequately. In most instances, you will want to have a portfolio with some investments that provide great financial returns in the short term, along with some that pay off over the longer term. Additionally, it is likely that the portfolio will have some investments that may not be particularly financially attractive but are made for strategic reasons. Finally, there is a risk spectrum that a corporate portfolio will likely span; that is, a large component of investments will likely be those that are less risky, but there will also be room for some portion of the portfolio allocated to riskier investments in areas such as innovation, technology, and the like.

Question 7: Do you capture a small number of core metrics that are tied to/drive the company's strategic plan? Are the metrics organizationally accepted?

Considerations: There is a metrics zeitgeist now. Measurement of any kind and translation into a metric is seen as a positive. There are scorecards, dashboards, cockpits, business intelligence applications, and reporting tools that all provide a panacea for what ails companies by allowing for the use of metrics. Ultimately these metrics are supposed to inform you about your progress against your strategies and drive your success. Fortunately, this is not all false; metrics are important. The problem in general is that either too many metrics are collected or they are the wrong metrics. The predicament created by too many metrics is that it creates noise. People do not know which are important, and linking these metrics to strategy becomes difficult and unwieldy. With too many metrics, you can always find a way to use them to show an investment in a good or a bad light. Initiative owners can disguise bad investments as good ones, or someone can question good investments by showing them in a bad light using some other metrics. Many times, the issue is that the wrong metrics are tracked and so the implications for strategy in this case can be dire if not remedied quickly. Sometimes the wrong metrics look only at short-term performance; as a result, the organization increasingly looks only at the short term with deleterious impact on the medium and long term.

Organizational Behavior

Question 1: What is the "personality" of your organization and how will CPM fit with this personality?

Considerations: CPM has a propensity to get under some people's skin. Because CPM is data driven and rigorous, it will, if done right, expose certain individuals and investments that are not worthy of resources. Some organizations do not like this. Organizations that rely heavily on the charisma, relationships, and intuition of a few people are tougher prospects for CPM, even though they are likely to be more in need of CPM. If information silos are significant and the distribution of information and knowledge is not happening or encouraged, CPM is also difficult. This does not mean it is impossible, but knowing where an organization stands from a personality perspective is important in providing a sense for how much work will be required to implant CPM. If your organization is data driven and is one in which knowledge is distributed and politics are minimal, there is a better foundation for CPM.

Question 2: What is the "political landscape" of your organization?

Considerations: Analysis of whether to implement CPM cannot be relegated to the numbers and data. While organizational politics is something the vast majority wishes was avoidable, the reality is that it exists; therefore, as you think about CPM, you should aim to identify who your fellow promoters/ allies and senior-level champions might be. Just as important, you should begin to identify the detractors who may wish to impede or even torpedo CPM as well as who the potential independents are who truly have no pre-set view of CPM; hopefully you can persuade them to join your camp in support of CPM. In many organizations, investment decisions and resource allocation can be highly politicized, so as you embark on the development of a CPM capability, it is important to understand these organizational realities and enter with your eyes open.

Question 3: How much time do you have to develop CPM within the organization (i.e., what is your organization's patience level)?

Considerations: Generally, you and your management will and should want results sooner than later. Constructing a rock-solid CPM capability, if not a marathon as previously mentioned, is definitely a half-marathon. If there are expectations that CPM will deliver appreciable results in a short time-frame (less than 18 months for large organizations), expectations may be too aggressive. As a result, several things may happen.

- The process is suboptimally architected in order to push CPM forward in an unrealistic timeframe.
- When CPM ultimately does not happen within the aggressive time-frame, it loses some of its credibility, not because of its fundamental characteristics but because of the inability to deliver it so quickly.
- People spearheading the CPM initiative can get disillusioned with the process as they are pushing ahead in a timeframe that is too aggressive, which will, in turn, impact the ultimate value that CPM delivers.

It is important to have pragmatic expectations and timelines to make CPM happen. After all, it is a change management exercise and change in many organizations requires education, internal syndication, process development—and all these take time. A measured pace is best, as it allows enough time to make a contribution while pushing CPM leaders to make progress and show results. In the rare instance where CPM is given too much time to show success, there is a danger that the initiative will become irrelevant or fall out of organizational consciousness before it even shows any results.

Even with a measured pace, it is still reasonable to expect interim milestones to be delivered that will show the progress of CPM and that benefit the organization. Interim milestones may include the reengineering or creation of driver-based models, the determination of what metrics will be employed, and the specific determination and definition of what is considered an investment. Achieving these will demonstrate progress as you work toward developing a more holistic CPM capability.

Question 4: Is cross-organizational/functional sharing of information occurring and encouraged?

Considerations: Successful CPM requires organizational openness and transparency. If your organization is already sharing information and has built a culture of openness and knowledge transfer, this will make CPM easier to implement. In organizations where this type of information exchange is not part of the prevailing temperament, some people may be uneasy with CPM, given that it requires a level of information sharing, introspection and transparency which will be unfamiliar. The understanding and assessment of how well your organization distributes knowledge provides a guide as to how much ongoing education and involvement the group coordinating CPM will have to do (i.e., the more siloed information is within an organization, the more continual effort will be required). Whether an organization is evolved or unevolved with regard to its information sharing, implementing CPM will likely cause some growing pains or a short-term regression in this sharing. Selecting the best investments from across the organization means the creation of a competitive marketplace for investments, and with this competition for funding will likely come some reticence to share information. These short-term blips are to be expected, because this type of constructive conflict for investment dollars is ultimately in the organization's best interest.

Question 5: Are incentives (compensation, promotion, etc) aligned and configured in a way that promotes total organization success over individual (i.e., unit, product, and geographic) success? And do incentives consider short- and long-term organizational aspirations?

Considerations: If individuals see their compensation and career opportunities tied to the results of particular subunits, products, or markets, and not to the overall success of the organization, their willingness to allocate resources to the best opportunities across the organization is inhibited. This obviously hinders CPM progress. When comparing a subset of investments across the organization to determine which to fund, aligning people's interests with those of the total organization is essential to ensure that people do not inflexibly fight for their group's investments and instead pick the best investments for the organization. The expectation of aligning incentives is not that one or two actions by individuals will provide the solution to managing the corporate portfolio, but that many individual actions will help move the organization to a superior corporate portfolio. Aligning incentives to consider total organization performance does not imply that individual results are not important. In fact, most people within an organization can do little on an individual basis to influence total organizational behavior, and their most important role, in fact, is to achieve the results that they have promised for their individual investments. But some aspect of total organizational performance must be considered as a material part of employee incentives to ensure the realization of CPM benefits.

Attitude and Readiness

Question 1: How much would CPM (if done right) help your organization and/or company?

Considerations: If you do not believe that CPM will have major positive implications for your organization, you should reconsider CPM. Implementing CPM can be time consuming and requires resources, and because it is not a quick hit that will happen across the organization in a few weeks or months, you should expend the energy on CPM only if the organization feels the benefits will be material. Doing CPM right is obviously important in this equation. Implementing a bad process and not properly aligning organizational behavior will handicap the ultimate impact of CPM and will also tarnish your personal credibility if you are the leader of the initiative. Additionally, the failure of any initial CPM effort will impede any future effort to optimize the corporate portfolio; consequently, even though it may be the right thing for the organization, confidence, due to a bad effort, will diminish and ultimately turn decision makers sour on trying again.

Question 2: How big of an undertaking is CPM within your organization?

Considerations: This question does not drive whether you should or should not pursue a CPM strategy. It just forces someone advocating CPM to understand how much effort will be required, and, more importantly, to ask whether the organization is willing to expend that much effort. It is likely that the requisite organizational behavior and process are not currently present or perhaps, for fortunate organizations, that one of these key levers may be in place. But moving either lever is going to be arduous. Process alignment is generally easier than behavioral modification, so if your organization is already behaviorally onboard or committed to the idea of CPM and just needs to fill in the process elements around it, you are in much better shape. However, if the converse is true and organizational behavior is what needs to be adjusted, this can be a more challenging task. It is vital to take an inventory of where the organization stands today to develop a good plan for implementing CPM and ensure that you are setting realistic expectations and timelines for CPM.

Question 3: Do you have a senior-level CPM champion within the organization?

Considerations: In the organizations chronicled for case studies in this book, one of the single most important items required for CPM success is a senior-level champion of the initiative. The best-case scenario is that you, the promoter of CPM, are also the senior-level leader, as this obviously makes CPM a much easier organizational sell. If you are not the senior-level leader but have access to the ear of a senior-level leader or group of leaders who can provide essential support and air cover for this initiative, you are also in a firm starting position. Before you embark on CPM, ensure that you have the champion in place. There are myriad change management efforts going on within an organization at any moment, and all of them are probably looking for senior advocates. And in all likelihood, they may be "targeting" the same advocates for their initiatives as you. So it is very important to create a solid business rationale and case in order to procure the support of a champion before driving toward CPM.

It is also important to consider the quality of your senior-level sponsorship. This is not a reference to the quality of the senior leader, as the hope is that you have been astute enough to get a champion who is respected within the organization. The extent to which the senior-level leader is actively engaged in making CPM a reality is important and is what is meant by "quality" of senior-level sponsorship. If your presentation to a prospective champion elicits "This is good stuff. Go ahead and do it and let me know what you find out," you do not have a committed senior-level champion. You have someone who is viewing this as an experiment and who may get committed down the road if the fruit from the experiment is sufficiently sweet. A committed senior-level champion gets involved in CPM and does not just say "let's do it"; instead, he says "I want to do this. What do you need from me?" or "I want to do this. Here is what I'd like to see." It is critical that the champion offer up his own time and ideas to promote CPM. If the senior-level leader offers aggressive cross-organizational goals tied to CPM, this is a good place to be. For example, "I'd like to see each business unit moving toward a CPM discipline by creating driver-based models before the end of the year" is a great actionable priority and goal that can then be used to demonstrate the commitment to drive CPM forward. Ideally, if CPM goals can be intertwined with individual goals and incentives, a tangible metric has been put in place to incentivize the adoption of CPM within the organization. TransUnion, American Express, Hewlett-Packard (HP), and others all had senior leaders actively engaged with and promoting the CPM discipline within their organizations which ultimately helped to drive the success of these programs.

A word of caution at this point. Although the champion is important, relying solely on a champion to make CPM happen is not realistic. Top-down support is important, but it is just as crucial to gather support from the bottom up as well; these are the people who ultimately will be doing the heavy lifting. If the basis for why they should participate is "Because [fill in name of champion here] said so," this justification for CPM will wear thin over time. Those listening to this rationale for CPM have the potential to go from being engaged to being actively disengaged over time; therefore, it is important to ensure that you continue to garner their support for CPM on an ongoing basis.

Question 4: Are there any potential quick but material wins for CPM (e.g., are there specific areas of the company that CPM can be developed in) to provide you and the effort with appropriate credibility and momentum?

Considerations: Momentum is crucial in any change-management effort, and CPM is no different. Saying that we will start implementing CPM today and will be back in 24 months with some results is not going to suffice. There is an inherent and underlying tendency to ask "What have you done for me lately?" within an organization, and to this end, finding a quick win or two for CPM is indispensable as you attempt to build up some brand equity for CPM and yourself. These wins are important because

- They let you fend off detractors who do not like CPM.
- They make your champion look good.
- They create other promoters who can help evangelize about CPM.
- They show the rest of the organization the power of CPM.

Once you have some wins, there is the challenge of letting people know. The old "if a tree falls in the forest and there is nobody around, does it make a sound" conundrum applies loosely here as well. Having wins and not telling anyone about them does not do you any good. You need to advertise your wins in some way. This does not mean mounting an aggressive internal public relations campaign or engaging in self-important conversations about how CPM has saved parts of the organization. It does mean talking about these wins as you pursue the implementation of CPM, and if possible, enlisting the beneficiaries of these wins to help you to sell CPM. The people who actually benefited from CPM can be powerful advocates of CPM because they can be viewed as more impartial than an individual or group tasked with making CPM a reality.

It is important to notice the term "material wins" in this question. Showing that CPM can work on a unit or product that most others consider immaterial or unlike the rest of the company is not going to induce support or excitement around CPM. You need to pick an area that is material—either in size or in significance—so that people will take notice. For example, if you have an organization with two large business units that make up 98% of the company's revenues and net income but you enable CPM in a third unit that is, for all practical purposes, a "rounding error," the reaction will range from a prolonged yawn to active disinterest, with comments like "It's easy to use CPM on those guys. They look nothing like us in terms of business model or complexity." So as you consider the wins, think about materiality. Do not experiment with CPM in an area people will not care about. You will spend lots of energy for little upside. Areas that are large and where there are significant issues are the best places to enable CPM. That said, challenged areas are often dealing with more pressing basic concerns, so implementing CPM may not be a top priority for them.

Question 5: What type of resources (people and/or money) will you have to deploy to make CPM a reality?

Considerations: You cannot make CPM a reality on your own (although it can be done relatively inexpensively), so understanding what resources you have or will have is crucial. If you already have a team that can work, even part-time to start, on CPM, you are in decent shape. The resources are important to manage the many CPM workstreams and to also provide a second or third perspective on your thinking. In your fervor to make CPM happen, sometimes you will fail to see certain obstacles that can sideswipe your efforts. Having some other voices will help strengthen the overall CPM business case and effort.

Question 6: If CPM is something you are advocating and something you hope to spearhead, what are your personal ambitions and hopes as they relate to CPM?

Considerations: Jim Collins, author of *Built to Last* and *Good to Great*, would call CPM for an entire organization a BHAG—a big hairy audacious goal. You are asking people to change decision making and even to forego their own interests at times for the benefit of the organization. Noble intentions underlie CPM, but achieving it is easier said than done. And given these challenges, you, if you are the main promoter or leader of this effort, must understand the challenges that lie before you.

If CPM is not going to help you in your career, then it does not pass the litmus test for "enlightened self-interest." You need to ensure that you will benefit from the success of CPM. This will ensure your own commitment to CPM as obstacles emerge. It will also ensure that CPM is architected properly for the organization as you will be personally invested in its success.

Once you have understood these dimensions related to organizational behavior, process and discipline and readiness and attitude, you are ready to engage in a thorough analysis of your organization's overall readiness for CPM. Based on your answers and thoughts as they relate to these questions, you may determine that implementing CPM is the way to go, and. if so, the next phase is galvanizing support. Keep in mind that many of the facts uncovered in the analyze phase are useful data points as you build the case and support for CPM.

Exhibit 2.2 provides a sample questionnaire pertaining to Step 1, Analyze.

EXHIBIT 2.2   **SURVEY TO ANALYZE YOUR ORGANIZATION'S CPM CAPABILITIES AND READINESS**

Step 1: Analyze
PROCESS AND DISCIPLINE

	Scoring	Today	Aspiration
1. How do you currently manage your company's investments?			
Rigor			
Investments are modeled using driver-based models.	3		
Investment models tend to be nondriver based and more back-of-the-envelope, relying on business experience and instinct.	2		
We do not model investments but rely on a combination of experience, intuition, and management direction to determine where to invest.	1		
Standardization			
We use standardized driver-based investment models to value investments.	3		
We use standardized non-driver based investment models.	2		

EXHIBIT 2.2   CONTINUED

	Scoring	Today	Aspiration
Modeling is done by subject matter experts and can vary based on their view of their business.	1		
We do not model investments using a consistent methodology.	0		

Data availability

Information on investments is collected across the organization and aggregated to enable knowledge-sharing and comparison of projects.	2		
There is no process to collect investment information from across the organization.	0		

Centralization of assumptions

Certain key assumptions are centralized and monitored to ensure consistency across investment models.	2		
Guidance is issued on certain key assumptions, but there is no means in place to ensure this.	1		
There are no central assumptions presently.	0		

2. Is there an organizational nerve center that people who may be competing for resources will believe? If this group came out with cross-organization recommendations related to the portfolio, would they be viewed as unbiased and credible?

There is a group within the organization that can do this and that has the requisite skills and credibility.	3		
There is a group within the organization that can do this and has the requisite skills. Decision makers may need to be sold on this, however.	2		
There currently is not a group within the organization like this.	0		

3. What is the evolution of investment tracking within the organization?

Tracking performance

Automated tracking systems exist that capture actual investment performance and enable comparison of projections and actuals (i.e., promise versus performance).	5		

(continues)

EXHIBIT 2.2   CONTINUED

	Scoring	Today	Aspiration
Automated tracking systems exist that capture actual investment performance, but currently, there is no means to compare projections and actual results.	4		
Automated tracking systems exist that capture aggregated performance results. These may enable comparison of projections and actuals at some level, but it may not be at an individual investment level.	3		
Tracking systems vary with some being automated and some being offline. The level of granularity available to track investments varies significantly and is not fully known.	1		
Tracking systems are not in place.	0		

Complexity of tracking infrastructure

	Scoring	Today	Aspiration
We have a few central systems that track actuals.	5		
We have many systems that track actuals.	3		
We use ad hoc methods to track actuals.	1		
Actuals tracking is not a key priority, and hence we do not know this.	0		

4. What is deemed an investment within your organization?

	Scoring	Today	Aspiration
We think many discretionary areas fall into the investment category, and we have a good definition for what is or is not an investment.	5		
We think many discretionary areas can be deemed investments, but we do not have a clear definition outlining what is and is not an investment.	3		
Many areas of investment spending are considered business as usual, and we have a limited number of items that would be deemed investments.	1		
We do not have a definition for what is an investment.	0		

5. Is there a rigorously created and followed formal organizational strategic plan that serves as the basis for people's actions, goals, and so on?

	Scoring	Today	Aspiration
There is a formal strategic plan in place that is followed and that does determine the objectives for the organization.	5		

EXHIBIT 2.2   CONTINUED

	Scoring	Today	Aspiration
There is a formal strategic plan in place, but it is often changed based on changing priorities and needs.	3		
There is not an organizationwide strategic plan in place as various subgroups (business units, functional groups, geographies, etc.) create their own individual strategies, which they follow.	1		
We do not have a formalized organizational or subgroup strategic plan in place.	0		

6. Is there a utilized framework in place to evaluate the risk associated with investments?

	Scoring	Today	Aspiration
We have a robust risk framework in place that considers operational, credit, and market risk, which are actively considered when making investment decisions.	5		
We consider risk when making investment decisions, but we do not have a codified means of assessing risk.	3		
Our focus when making investment decisions is on strategic and financial returns, with risk not being a major consideration.	1		

7. Do you measure a small number of core metrics that are tied to and drive the company's strategy/ strategic plan? Are the metrics organizationally accepted?

	Scoring	Today	Aspiration
We measure a small number of core metrics that are linked to and drive organizational strategy. People within the organization use these metrics in developing strategies, framing their discussions and tracking performance.	5		
We measure a small group of core metrics to understand how we are tracking against expectations, but there is only a loose or minimal tie to strategy. People within the organization use these metrics in tracking performance mainly.	3		
We measure a large group of core metrics to understand how our organization is doing against many sets of expectations, but there is only a loose or minimal tie to strategy. People within the organization use some of these metrics as requisite.	2		

(continues)

EXHIBIT 2.2   CONTINUED

	Scoring	Today	Aspiration
We measure many metrics that people within the organization use for different purposes. People use metrics as required.	1		
We measure few to no metrics or we measure too many metrics. There is no widespread organizational understanding of these metrics, and their utilization is uncertain.	0		

Max score = 43, Min Score = 2

Step 1: Analyze
ORGANIZATIONAL BEHAVIOR

	Scoring	Today	Aspiration
1. What is the "personality" of your organization, and how will CPM fit with this personality?			
We are a data-driven culture that relies on hard data to make decisions.	5		
We use data when available, but we do not generally need or collect data to make decisions, as a sound qualitative strategy or business case is sufficient.	3		
We prefer our gut instinct and experience over analysis using data.	0		
2. What is the "political landscape" of your organization?			
We do not have organizational silos. Communication and collaboration are fostered across the organization.	3		
Organizational silos exist but are being broken down. There is a willingness by senior management to break these down.	1		
Our organization is highly siloed with clear demarcation between various silos and autonomy across silos. Communication and collaboration within the organization are inhibited by silos.	0		
3. How much time do you have to develop CPM within the organization (i.e., what is your organization's patience level)?			
Measured—Show demonstrable results in the next 6 to 18 months	5		

EXHIBIT 2.2   CONTINUED

	Scoring	Today	Aspiration
Over time—Show demonstrable results in 18+ months	3		
Aggressive—Show demonstrable results in the next 6 to 12 months	1		

4. Is cross-organizational or cross-functional sharing of information occurring and encouraged?

	Scoring	Today	Aspiration
It occurs in formal (through planned meetings, systems, etc.) and informal ways and is part of the culture of our organization. It is considered critical to our success.	3		
There are either formal or informal means by which information is shared across the organization. Knowledge sharing is good but not critical.	1		
Information tends to reside in silos within our organization and knowledge sharing is not a top priority.	0		

5. Are incentives (compensation, promotion, etc.) aligned and configured in a way that promotes total organization success over individual (i.e., unit, product, and geographic success)? And do incentives consider short- and long-term organizational aspirations?

	Scoring	Today	Aspiration
Incentives are in place that promote decision making that is in the interest of the total organization, and they aim to balance short- and long-term priorities.	5		
Incentives are in place that reward individual group, geography, and functional performance primarily, with overall short- and long-term organization performance also figuring into incentives.	2		
Incentives are generally aligned around individual performance, whether in a business segment, product group, functional area, geography, and so on, and total organization performance is not heavily considered or not considered at all or short-term performance is the priority over the long-term.	0		

Max = 26, min = 1

(continues)

EXHIBIT 2.2   CONTINUED

Step 1: Analyze
ATTITUDE AND READINESS

	Scoring	Today	Aspiration
1. How much would CPM (if done right) help your organization and/or company?			
Significant benefits	5		
Modest benefits	3		
Uncertain benefits	0		
2. How big of an undertaking is CPM in your estimation within your organization?			
Process and organizational behavior are well positioned for a move to CPM.	5		
Behavior alignment will be easier than the process.	3		
Process alignment will be easier than changing organizational behavior.	2		
Major behavior and process changes need to happen to enable CPM.	0		
3. Do you have a senior-level CPM champion within the organization?			
I have the influence to make CPM happen.	5		
I have some influence and access to the ear of potential CPM champions who see or will see the benefit of CPM.	3		
I do not have the influence myself but feel strongly that I could find the requisite people with influence.	2		
I do not have the influence and have not determined who the potential influencers are.	0		

EXHIBIT 2.2 CONTINUED

	Scoring	Today	Aspiration

4. Are there any potential quick but material wins for CPM (i.e., are there specific areas of the company that CPM can be developed in to provide you and the effort with appropriate credibility and momentum)?

	Scoring		
Several potential areas for quick material wins have been identified where CPM can be deployed to build credibility and momentum.	5		
There is one major area that could serve as a material win for CPM.	3		
There are several smaller areas in which CPM could be deployed to get a win.	1		
There is uncertainty about where CPM would be deployed at the organization to begin with.	0		

5. What type of resources (people and/or money) will you have to deploy and make CPM a reality?

	Scoring		
I have an organization that can work on CPM as requisite.	5		
It depends on me and my ability to "sell" the idea within the organization to determine the resources I will get.	3		
I need to prove the worth of CPM on my own, leveraging existing resources as possible.	1		

6. If CPM is something you are advocating and you hope to spearhead, what are your personal ambitions and hopes as they relate to CPM?

	Scoring		
If successful, CPM would help me build my personal brand within the organization.	3		
CPM is part of my job, and it could help me if it is successful.	1		
CPM, if successful, would not help or hurt me significantly.	0		

Max = 28, Min = 1

(continues)

EXHIBIT 2.2 CONTINUED

Scoring

After going through the questionnaire, see what your process and discipline as well as organizational behavior scores are today and see what box your scores put you into (see below). Following the discussion of these scores below, we will look at your organizational attitude and readiness scores to determine where your organization stands.

Score

		2–20	21–38	39–43
Process & Discipline → / Organizational Behavior ↓				
	19–21	4	7	9
	9–18	2	5	8
	1–8	1	3	6

Here is a breakdown of what these scores imply:

Boxes	Evolution Stage of CPM	What this means?
1, 2 or 3	Unconsciously Incompetent	• You are a visionary within your company, as most do not see CPM as necessary or essential. • In fact, most have not even heard of CPM. • There are probably significant benefits to be accrued from CPM if your organization can be awakened to its potential impacts. • It, however, will be a long, often hard, road to work from this evolutionary stage to the next, as there is significant effort required to move both behavior and process.

EXHIBIT 2.2   CONTINUED

Boxes	Evolution Stage of CPM	What this means?
4 or 6	Delusional	• This is a new stage that the prior framework did not address. • Because of the interdependencies between organizational behavior and process, it is virtually impossible to be so evolved on one dimension and so unevolved on another. • The dimensions move to some degree together. If you are in boxes 4 or 6, either you are selling yourself short on one dimension or being too generous on another.
5	Consciously Incompetent	• You have just moved into consciously incompetent category by virtue of your initial strides in behavior and process. • It is easy to regress into unconscious incompetence, so be careful in this stage.
7 or 8	Consciously Incompetent	• You have made major strides in behavior or process. • CPM is already, perhaps accidentally, happening within your organization. • Moving to conscious competence is a very challenging prospect as you have probably already tackled the major issues and now you will have to go after challenges that have deeper roots and for which the benefits are more incremental.
9	Consciously Competent	• You are highly evolved on both process and behavior and a rarity within larger organizations. • You must continue to push and reinforce both areas because regressing back to conscious incompetence is quite easy.

After compiling your scores for behavior and process and determining which box you are in, now consider your attitude and readiness scores using the following combined scoring framework.

(continues)

EXHIBIT 2.2 CONTINUED

Behavior and Process Box

Readiness and Attitude Score	1, 2 or 3	5	7 or 8	9
1–7	Stop	Proceed with caution	Proceed with caution	NA
8–14	Proceed with caution	Proceed with caution	Go	Go
15–21	Go	Go	Go	Go
22–28	Go	Accelerate	Accelerate	Accelerate

You will notice that boxes 4 and 6 are not considered in the above matrix given their implausibility.

What this means?

Action	Why?
Stop	• In this case, you have lots of work to do on process and behavior, which is difficult enough. • That challenge is being compounded with a lack of organizational readiness and attitude for CPM. • This is a road fraught with lots of headaches for which there is little payout. • CPM may be something you wish to revisit later on as the organization's behavior or process elements evolve a bit more.
Proceed with caution	• When organizational readiness and attitude are not abysmal but not great, it is important to take a pragmatic and measured approach to CPM. • If you are in this category, finding a credible senior level champion and a quick material win(s) for CPM are important, as these will give the initiative a stronger foundation on which to stand.
Go	• The attitude and readiness or the process and behavior are strong enough in this case to withstand some shocks, and so the focus in these instances is on execution. • Leverage your champion and/or wins already achieved to promote and expand the reach of CPM.
Accelerate	• You have solid behavior and processes for CPM coupled with organizational readiness and attitude, so leverage this to build momentum for CPM within the organization. • Continue to keep CPM as a top priority within the organization by referring back to the portfolio and the impacts to that portfolio through the CPM work being conducted.

EXHIBIT 2.2   CONTINUED

Action	Why?
NA	• Not applicable • It is not possible to be so evolved from an organizational process and behavior perspective and have such a poor organizational attitude or readiness.

The scores you indicate in the aspiration column, if very different from your today score may also provide useful insights into how much your organization wants and needs CPM. But be careful not to pursue CPM solely based on aspirations.

Note: The aim of this questionnaire is to gauge your beliefs about your organization's current process and behavior as it relates to corporate portfolio management (CPM) and also indicate where you would like to be with regard to CPM in the future. Your analysis should be an inventory of what you have in place today and should not consider your plans and goals. Your plans and goals are considered in the score you provide in the "Aspiration" column. This is a questionnaire best done by a small number of people in determining your organization's readiness for CPM, and these people will, in all likelihood, be actively involved in building a CPM capability if it goes forward. The questions are fairly specific, and in order for it to be useful, you must provide your honest and realistic assessment of where you are today and provide your realistic aspiration of where you would like to go.

Step 2: Galvanize

Once you have concluded the analyze phase and have determined that CPM will be beneficial for your organization, the next critical step is to galvanize support for this effort throughout the organization. Galvanizing support means appealing to the emotional and unemotional motivations people have, understanding the problems and issues they face, and addressing them. Before building your finalized business case for CPM, capture all the relevant feedback and garner support along the way by doing several things.

Leverage Your Champion   Why? Most obviously, you should utilize your champion because champions have power. And when someone in the organization who has power talks about CPM, it gives the effort credibility and momentum. Additionally, your champion has the ear of other senior leaders within the organization as well as employees throughout the organization who can help you make your case. Enlist their help, and you will be able to make significant strides in CPM in a more time-efficient manner.

How? There are several things your champion can do to make your push for CPM easier including

- **Talking about it.** Whether it is in small meetings or larger group or organization town halls, talking about CPM reinforces that this is an important initiative.

- **Making people responsible for it.** If possible, encourage the leader to set aggressive goals and timelines with regard to CPM. And once you have the champion's sign-off on these objectives, ensure that the champion promotes and discusses these expectations with others within the organization. Doing this creates momentum for CPM by building CPM-related activities into the goals of the organization.

- **Having it drive compensation.** This is related to the preceding point, but if there are goals tied to CPM, the next logical push is to build these into compensation and incentive structuring. There is not a better way to promote CPM than to have it tied to the personal bottom line of those in the organization. This is also clearly amongst the hardest things to do.

Build a Coalition   Why? As much as you would like to, you cannot change things by yourself. You need a group of fellow promoters who share your vision and passion and belief in CPM.

How? Having those who share your vision and passion for CPM is easier said than done especially as it relates to passion. Although you may be able to convince people of your vision and the pragmatic benefits of CPM, imbuing them with the same passion can be a daunting task. Methods to do this include

- **Brainstorming with your potential coalition.** Do not go with your business case for CPM preconstructed when talking about CPM with potential allies. Talking them through an explanation of what CPM is (if they do not already know) and explaining what you feel the merits and benefits of CPM would be is important, but only at a high level. Be sure that the benefits you outline are not all about the total organization; you need to show your potential coalition members what is in it for them. Do not make this a one-way exchange, with you expounding on the merits of CPM while they listen. Engage them in a conversation and ask questions. If possible, connect with the right people in that organization to conduct a brainstorming session where you try to uncover their thoughts on:

- What can be improved about current resource allocation decisions? Either across the company or within their unit?

- What challenges do they currently face, either in terms of process or behavior, in evaluating their own portfolio of investments?

- What is their current process for making investment decisions?

- How do they feel CPM might benefit them or the entire organization?

- What do they dislike or are uncertain about in connection with CPM?

Following this session, refine your business case for CPM by leveraging the thoughts, ideas, and challenges offered during these brainstorming sessions. People will appreciate the fact that their challenges and questions are being considered in the development of the CPM discipline, and ideally they will see that CPM will benefit them as well as the organization overall. By understanding what they do not like about CPM, you can hopefully develop a plan that addresses and resolves many of these issues.

- **Giving coalition members access to the champion.** Sometimes access to the champion, which can be highly coveted in some organizations, is a way to further support for CPM by potential coalition members. They will see CPM as more useful to them as they begin to realize that it can improve their own standing and recognition within the organization.

Do Not Confront or Embarrass Detractors   Why not? Because even the largest organizations have people separated by only two to three degrees; therefore, confronting or embarrassing detractors has the potential of coming back to bite you later on. Additionally, CPM is ultimately about inclusion, so be sure to spend initial time focusing on people who may become promoters of CPM and not those who are not advocates. That said, if a detractor does assail you or the benefits of CPM, you should vigorously defend CPM—just be sure that your counterattacks stick to the subject. After winning over promoters or those who are neutral on CPM, you can turn your mind to the critics. By this point, you have probably built up enough credibility for CPM that either the critics will fall in line or their nay-saying will backfire, making them appear unnecessarily obstinate.

Win Small, Win Early, Win Often   Why? Because momentum matters. So winning a particular business unit over or implementing CPM in a part of the organization with favorable results is important to advertise. It gives CPM credibility.

Understand Challenges   Why? Do not assume that you are smart enough to know on your own how CPM can benefit the company.

How? As mentioned, talk to potential coalition members about their challenges. Understand your CPM champion's challenges and how CPM addresses these challenges. Also talk to people "in the trenches" of the organization to understand their thoughts on CPM and the current challenges they face. Their challenges may often be less about strategy and may focus more on the process and operational challenges they have. If their challenge with CPM is "who is going to do all the work associated with it?," you need to develop a good answer for this. Cataloging all these various pain points within the organization is important because you should aim to address these concerns in your CPM plan.

Do Best-Practices or Competitor Research on CPM   Why? This is not a must have, but if your organization likes to know what leading or competitor companies are doing with reference to CPM, it is worth documenting and benchmarking.

How? Information to this end is not readily available, given the newness of CPM. Still, you can leverage the burgeoning group of consultants and software companies in the emerging portfolio management arena. While they are pitching you for work, you can often find out interesting bits of information from them about other companies using CPM. Be careful, however, of any "best practices" you see discussed. This is a relatively new area of study, so true best practices are few and far between. Instead of holding yourself to some fictional best-practice standard, aim to be the developer of best practices within your own organization.

Augment Business Case with Information That Demonstrates Knowledge of CPM   Why? If you are going to be the brains behind CPM, you need to demonstrate that you understand CPM.

How? Leverage available resources to constantly increase your understanding of CPM. See the Appendices for useful information and figures which can be used for your CPM business case.

Determine the Return on Investment of CPM   Why? Because CPM is about data-driven decisions, eating one's own dog food and understanding the bottom-line impact, even at a high-level, for CPM is important.

How? While modeling the benefits of CPM can be done very rigorously, what follows is a very high-level method of approximating the return on investment (ROI) of CPM. As you will see, CPM's ROI is not predicated on cost savings or productivity enhancements. It is based on an assumption that discretionary investments from across the organization will be more efficiently selected and will perform better. The steps are outlined as follows:

Step 1: How large is the discretionary expense base that you are considering for CPM? If you do not have a number in mind, a fair approximation is to take your operating expense budget and assume that somewhere between 30 to 40% is discretionary.

Step 2: What is the average payback period of investments? Of course, most portfolios will have some investments that pay back almost immediately along with other multi-year investments that take several years to pay back. This will depend on your industry and the nature of your investments. If your investments are in mining or manufacturing, for example, the paybacks are longer than investments in direct marketing. Of course, there are investments that have uncertain or indeterminable paybacks. Assume the payback of such investments is a sufficiently long period and develop a weighted-average approximation of payback. Take a two- to four-year payback as average, depending on your industry.

Step 3: What is the rate your discretionary investment funding pool is growing at, year over year? Given the reengineering that is going on, do not assume that drops in operating expense mean reductions in discretionary investment spending. In all likelihood, total expenses may be down as a result of productivity and efficiency savings, but discretionary investments may be up or flat, as these are what really drive business growth. In highly competitive industries this amount will grow faster year over year than in more stable, old-line industries. The growth range you can approximate if you do not have better numbers is 5 to 15%.

With these three steps, you now have enough to build a quick model for implementing CPM. This is a high-level case so, depending on your audience, you should consider augmenting this with additional analysis.

The following is an example using a fictional company, with following assumptions being made:

Assumptions
($ in thousands)

Total operating expenses in year 1	$3,333	
Percent of OpEx that is discretionary	30%	
Discretionary investments in year 1	$1,000	
Growth in discretionary investments year over year	12%	yoy
Average investment cash flow payback period (yrs)	3	yrs

Without CPM, the investment performance over the next five years would look like this.

Pre-CPM Investment
Performance

($ thousands)	Year 1	Year 2	Year 3	Year 4	Year 5
Year 1 Investments	($1,000)	$333	$333	$333	$333
Year 2 Investments	$0	($1,120)	$373	$373	$373
Year 3 Investments	$0	$0	($1,254)	$418	$418
Year 4 Investments	$0	$0	$0	($1,405)	$468
Year 5 Investments	$0	$0	$0	$0	($1,574)
	($1,000)	($787)	($548)	($280)	$20

As you can see, there is an assumption that $1 million is the discretionary investment pool in year 1, which grows by 12% year over year (year 2 investment = $1M × 1.12), and this trend continues. Additionally, the cash flow generated in years 2 through 5 is the initial investment amount divided by the number of years until payback (i.e., $1M invested, which pays back over three years, generates $333,000 of cash flow in year 2 and so on).

Assuming CPM yields a 3% improvement in investment performance, this equates to cash flows post-CPM as follows:

Post-CPM Investment Performance ($ thousands)

	Year 1	Year 2	Year 3	Year 4	Year 5
Year 1 Investments	($1,000)	$343	$343	$343	$343
Year 2 Investments	$0	($1,120)	$385	$385	$385
Year 3 Investments	$0	$0	($1,254)	$431	$431
Year 4 Investments	$0	$0	$0	($1,405)	$482
Year 5 Investments	$0	$0	$0	$0	($1,574)
	($1,000)	($777)	($527)	($246)	$67

The incremental cash flow benefit in this case is as follows:

Impacts ($ thousands)

Investment cash flow pre-CPM	($1,000)	($787)	($548)	($280)	$20
Investment cash flow post-CPM	($1,000)	($777)	($527)	($246)	$67
Incremental cash flow as a result of CPM	$0	$10	$21	$34	$48
Total cumulative cash flow benefit	$113				

The improvements on various scenarios of improvement performance are as follows:

CPM improves investment performance by	5-year cumulative cash flow impact
1%	$38
2%	$75
3%	$113
4%	$150
5%	$188
6%	$225
7%	$263
8%	$300
9%	$338
10%	$375
11%	$413
12%	$450
13%	$488
14%	$525
15%	$563

As you can see, CPM offers significant benefits even with very modest assumptions relating to benefits. Even a 1% improvement in investment performance yields $38 million in cashflow in this high-level example. This can help in justifying the resources needed to make CPM a reality, given that very conservative improvement expectations offer significant benefit.

The example does not deal with projects that do not happen because of better investment decision making, but this, to some degree, is encapsulated in the improved investment performance of the portfolio. If you feel there are currently many investments within your organization that would not be selected or more rigorously reviewed on an ongoing basis to improve performance, your estimate for the improvement CPM will enable will be greater, making the economic case for CPM even more attractive.

The development of your initial CPM business case is important as you start moving toward CPM, but even if successful in making CPM happen, it is important to constantly galvanize support for CPM, and this means constantly pushing organizational behavior.

Change Organizational Behavior on an Ongoing Basis One of the things most apparent after talking to CPM practitioners is that ongoing education about CPM and its benefits is absolutely requisite in order to be successful. Attempts to change organizational behavior should be considered as you galvanize support for CPM within the organization. While much of your galvanization effort may be focused on getting senior advocates onboard who will help push adoption of CPM, you must also sell CPM in a bottom-up manner to "win the hearts and minds" of the people who will have to do much of the work to make this happen. Doing this requires thinking about organizational behavior. You will not change this overnight, but instead, your aim is to ensure that people know why they are doing CPM and understand what its benefits are for them and the organization.

Note that in the context of organizational behavior, aligning incentive compensation with long-term company goals and optimized portfolio management is not covered because this is incredibly complex and probably best not handled by someone pushing for CPM. Any time you suggest that senior leadership's payment mechanisms should be changed you will cause some heartburn. Although changing compensation to align with CPM is important over the long term, this is probably a battle best fought late in the game after CPM has gained significant momentum and has shown results.

So how does an organization go about effectively educating its employees about CPM. While there is no right answer, there are two specific examples that are worth highlighting as typical of organizations that are thinking ahead in these areas and that offer ideas that you may want to adapt within your organization to start pushing for changes in organizational behavior.

AMERICAN EXPRESS'S IO SUMMIT

In October 2005, American Express held its first ever CPM summit. The company invited about 100 personnel from around the world to New York for two intensive days of Investment Optimization (IO) specific learning and exercises (IO is American Express's term for CPM). The conference was coordinated by a central IO team within the company's corporate planning and analysis group. Beyond the content of the conference, the summit served as a means to get people from various business units, product groups, and geographies to network, exchange best practices, and so forth.

One of the central tenets of the conference was that although the IO effort started as a finance initiative, the initiative owners from the business (e.g., marketing, operations, sales, etc.), had to be active and engaged stakeholders in the IO process. To this end, they required that each business unit submitting potential attendees to the conference must have at least 25% of their prospective attendees be from the business.

The first sign of "success" was that the conference was over-subscribed from a demand perspective, and people actually had to be turned away. This was an early indication that other efforts to socialize IO within the organization were taking hold.

The agendas for each day are shown in Exhibit 2.3 so you can see the types of activities that were planned. One of the main principles behind the summit was that this should be an interactive conference where people were "not talked at" for eight hours but were engaged to think about CPM. Additionally, the idea was to highlight external thought-leaders' ideas on topics of interest and to share best practices that units had developed. As you can see, although the corporate IO group pulled the conference together, the aim was to give the

(continues)

conference many voices. Of course, senior-level engagement and participation in the conference was present, with the Senior Vice President of
Corporate Planning and Analysis, Alan Gallo, attending throughout and
opening the conference. Additionally, the company's CFO, Gary Crittenden, addressed the attendees, highlighting the importance of IO to the
overall company.

It is apparent from the foregoing agenda that this was a very busy
time for attendees. Two of the things that American Express
presented at the conference, beyond featuring the previously mentioned internal and external speakers, were (1) an awards ceremony
and (2) a portfolio-management simulation.

The awards ceremony was most obviously a great way to recognize the individuals who had really helped drive the IO discipline in
their organizations. This public acknowledgment of those people
who, at a grassroots level, make American Express's IO efforts successful was a great way to provide these individuals with high-level
exposure and to reenergize them with reference to the company's IO
imperatives.

The portfolio management simulation was a very interesting exercise that was self-constructed by the central IO team. The day 1 session was an exercise in which a fictional group of investments was
given to each group and each individual on the team was assigned a
specific functional role or type of investment (IT, customer acquisition, brand/loyalty, operations). Each of them was given the following
scenario to set the stage for day 1:

- **The good news.** Because of outstanding performance, an incremental $15M of investment funding has become available to
  your business unit.
- **What has been done?** Each functional group in your business
  unit has been solicited for its list of unfunded investments (list
  you have).
- **The dilemma.** You have an incremental $15M of funding, and
  you have received unfunded investment proposals totaling
  $30M.
- **What is left to do?** In order to work through this dilemma, your
  business unit has convened a rapid action investment decision-
  ing (RAID) team. The goal of the RAID team is to work together
  to develop a joint recommendation on which initiatives will
  receive the funding.

EXHIBIT 2.3   AMERICAN EXPRESS CPM SUMMIT AGENDA

Day 1 Agenda

Timing	Description
730–845 am	Breakfast & Registration
845–930 am	Opening Remarks
930–1000 am	Simulation instructions
1000–1200 pm	Breakout Sessions (Resource Allocation Simulation day 1)
1200–100 pm	Lunch
100–200 pm	IO system update and progress
200–245 pm	Business Unit Best Practices Spotlight: Investment Scoring and Prioritization
245–400 pm	External perspectives: Managing Customers as Investments (Professor)
400–415 pm	Break
415–515 pm	Resource Allocation Simulation Results Review
515–530 pm	Day One Wrap-up
600–645 pm	Cocktail Reception
645–830 pm	Dinner Reception & Awards Ceremony

Day 2 Agenda

730–830 am	Breakfast
830–900 am	Simulation instructions & overview
900–1040 am	Breakout: Resource Allocation Simulation (Part Two)
1040–1050 am	Break
1050–1200 pm	External Perspective: From Resource Allocation to Strategy (Professor)
1200–100 pm	Lunch
100–140 pm	Business Unit Best Practice Spotlight: Improving Loyalty Investment Effectiveness
140–250 pm	External Perspective: IT Investment Optimization (Bulge Bracket Consulting Company)
250–300 pm	Break
300–430 pm	Resource Allocation Simulation Results Review
430–500 pm	Closing Remarks

(continues)

- **Your role.** Each of you has been given a business unit and functional group that you will represent as part of the RAID team. You should keep in mind two equally important goals that you have. You want to ensure
- That your business unit selects the best unfunded investments.
- That the needs and goals of your functional group are represented in the selected investments.

This day 1 session focused each functional group on pushing for its investments while also trying to do what is best for the overall business. The aim was to drive home the complexity of portfolio management within a single unit and to show that doing what is right for one's functional area may lead to suboptimal decisions for the overall unit. The simulation also highlighted the applicability of CPM within a portion of the organization.

On day 2, an urgent fictitious memo was issued to each of the attendees with the following directive:

- **The good news.** Because of the sale of certain assets, an incremental $40M of investment funding has become available.
- **What has been done?** Each unit has been solicited for its list of unfunded investments (four lists you have).
- **The dilemma.** You have an incremental $40M of funding, but at a total organizational level, you have received unfunded investment proposals from the units totaling $120M.
- **What is left to do?** In order to work through this, senior management has asked that a cross-business unit investment review council (IRC) convene tomorrow morning to determine which investments should be funded.
- **Your role.** Each of you will attend the IRC as representatives of your unit and your unit's unfunded investments. You should keep in mind two important goals. You want to ensure
  - That you work with your peers from other units to determine the best unfunded investments from a total organizational perspective. Failing to put your company hat on will not be looked upon favorably by senior management.
  - That you adequately represent the objectives/investments of your unit. Failure to do this will reflect poorly upon you in the eyes of your unit president and unit management.

Day 2 differed from day 1 in that the goal today was not to represent your functional area but to represent your business unit and debate the merits of your unit's investments against those provided by other units. The information provided for all investments included financial, strategic, and risk elements. To further complicate things and provide a greater sense of reality, some of the information given for investments was not accurate.

Day 2 drove home the point again that CPM is an effort that can be utilized across business units. During the day's debrief, the central IO team who served as facilitators throughout the day compiled the results and showed the various teams how each group had decisioned the investments. It became apparent very quickly that there was no right answer and that different people and groups considered different factors in varying ways. This highlighted two main points: (1) IO is not a black box and (2) portfolio optimization across the organization yields better results than optimization within a single unit or functional area. The sample results are given in Exhibit 2.4.

EXHIBIT 2.4   SAMPLE RESULTS FROM CPM SIMULATION

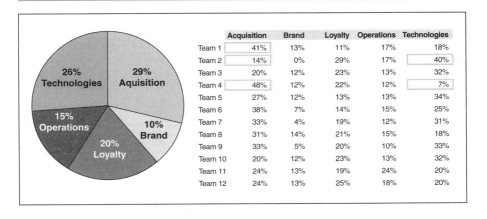

	Acquisition	Brand	Loyalty	Operations	Technologies
Team 1	41%	13%	11%	17%	18%
Team 2	14%	0%	29%	17%	40%
Team 3	20%	12%	23%	13%	32%
Team 4	48%	12%	22%	12%	7%
Team 5	27%	12%	13%	13%	34%
Team 6	38%	7%	14%	15%	25%
Team 7	33%	4%	19%	12%	31%
Team 8	31%	14%	21%	15%	18%
Team 9	33%	5%	20%	10%	33%
Team 10	20%	12%	23%	13%	32%
Team 11	24%	13%	19%	24%	20%
Team 12	24%	13%	25%	18%	20%

Pie chart: 29% Aquisition, 26% Technologies, 15% Operations, 20% Loyalty, 10% Brand

Another innovative way to change organizational behavior is through the use of formal educational programs. HP has developed some innovative practices in this regard.

HP's Strategic Financial Analysis Training

HP has developed a robust three-day training session that addresses strategic financial analysis and uses CPM as a backdrop to tie all the various tools and frameworks together. Creating awareness of CPM, especially among those new to the company, will prove to be beneficial as those people move within and up in the organization and think of CPM as a vital discipline. A more detailed view of what is covered in this training is given in the Appendix, but the high-level components are as follows:

- Introduction to Strategy and Decision Quality
- Framing Strategic Decisions
- Alternative Generation and Business Design
- Evaluating Decisions and Strategies under Uncertainty
- Probability Assessment
- Decision Criteria, Metrics, Probabilistic Analysis and Expected Value
- Putting It All Together: Excellence in Strategy Development
- Putting It All Together: Value-Based Portfolio Management

Step 3: Standardize

Once you have galvanized support for CPM, the task turns to standardizing how investments are viewed. The challenge here is getting different parts of the organization to talk the same language. Several questions need to be answered related to standardization including

- **Have we agreed on what a discretionary investment is?** This is the absolute most basic question that needs to be answered before you embark on CPM. As previously argued, be expansive in your definition of what is discretionary.

- **Which metrics are important and which are not?** Do not boil the ocean when it comes to metrics. Determine what drives your business performance and track those metrics. Ensure that there are metrics that are captured across the organization to enable comparability across investments.

- **How do we standardize modeling of investment projections?** Make certain that the metrics that are of interest are calculated similarly to ensure comparability across investments. In addition, working toward assumption standardization is equally important. There is no easy way to standardize modeling of investments. It requires collecting investment models and diving in deep to see how things are done. There is also a need to standardize across investment types (i.e., if different units have sales force investments having a similar methodology will be important). Additionally, moving to a driver-based standardized modeling standard is preferable because this enables more robust projection creation and more focused comparisons across investments.

- **What about investments that do not generate returns?** Many investments do not generate returns or produce returns that are easy to discern and capture. For example, loyalty investments may offer some benefits, but determining how much is due to the specific investment can be difficult. Nevertheless, these investments need to be considered in your CPM program, and there must be a way to capture consistent information about these investments as well. Since such investments are likely to have strategic benefits, these strategic considerations should be considered as you evaluate these investments. Additionally, the risk of these investments should be understood. Given their uncertain financial returns, it is very important to understand their riskiness. In many instances, these nonreturning investments are the first ones to be cut in difficult times; understanding the strategic and risk elements of these investments may help in supporting the need for them.

- **How do we collect this information?** The method by which investment information is collected really depends on the number of investments you are capturing. If the number is in the tens, simple modeling and aggregation via Excel will probably suffice. As your number of investments gets into the hundreds or even thousands, your methods of information collection need to get more sophisticated through the use of databases and reporting and analytics tools. But as previously discussed, be skeptical of the many portfolio-management tools on the market that promise the world but deliver very little. Focus first on your process and organizational behavior and then on the tool—not the other way around.

- **How often should we collect investment portfolio information?** While there is no standard or best practice on the number of times you should review investments, ensure that your investment review is happening more than once at the beginning of the year. This is one of the deadly sins of portfolio management, and treating CPM as a once-a-year exercise dooms your effort to failure. Your portfolio needs to be reviewed in a consistent, ongoing manner to understand the impacts of changing environments and priorities.

- **How do we compare actuals versus projections (e.g., promise versus performance)?** It is important to let investment owners know that they will be tasked with capturing actuals for their investments and that investments that cannot capture actuals but which promise benefits will be viewed with additional scrutiny. Setting aside a couple of checkpoints during the year to evaluate true investment performance is important because it enables a few key things to occur; specifically,

  - It promotes accountability.
  - It creates organizational learning.

  It is important to understand how investments are tracked as well. There are two types of investment tracking:

  1. **Capabilities-driven.** These are generally automated tracking systems that allow actuals to be captured on a recurring basis using a consistent methodology. This type of tracking is the most powerful as it can drive future investment projection creation using historical actual results, thereby creating the closed loop and organizational learning.

  2. **Ad hoc.** For certain types of investments, there is no way to track these investments using a system; consequently, more improvised methods of investment tracking must be employed. Using customer surveys, regression analyses, or other methods, some rudimentary and some very scientific, this type of investment tracking

tries to discern benefits based on extrapolations from collected information after the investment is actioned. This can be directionally useful, but many times this type of extemporized investment tracking is burdened with assumption-laden analysis that may be questionable. Additionally, this type of tracking does not create a repeatable process that can be used for projection creation going forward. While ad hoc tracking is potentially useful, capabilities-driven tracking is much more useful to an organization from a CPM perspective.

- **How do we evaluate qualitative factors such as risk and strategic benefit?** This is not easy. but building standardized frameworks for strategy and risk helps put investments on a level playing field with respect to these two important dimensions. Similar to standardizing modeling and metrics, when strategy and risk-evaluation frameworks are homogenized across the organization, it enables greater comparability of investments beyond just the numbers.

  Of course, the creation of a standard risk or strategic scoring method will require heavy amounts of collaboration and syndication within the organization. In addition, these frameworks cannot be used as some sort of universal remedy for evaluating risk and strategy. They are conversation starters—not conversation deciders.

Step 4: Optimize

You have analyzed the benefits and built a case for CPM, and as a result, you have galvanized support for it within the organization. Then you spent considerable time standardizing CPM methods across the organization and captured investment information from around the company. After all the blood, sweat, and tears, you are now ready to do what you set out to do—optimize your corporate portfolio.

With the exhilaration that comes with progressing this far, do not naively embark on a slash-and-burn-journey where you recommend investment cuts and reprioritizations based on the information you now have available before you. This is a quick way to turn CPM allies into enemies and throw your CPM efforts into a tailspin. Again, you need to remember what brought you this far—a consultative, data-driven process that created fellow advocates for CPM. Be careful not to disenchant those that have helped CPM (and you) become successful. There are a few different methods to improve and ultimately optimize your investment portfolio including

- Developing and utilizing a portfolio management framework or decision making tools that can be employed across at least some of the organization to help make investment recommendations
- Changing your organization's investment funding mechanism or process in a way that impacts resource allocation and, as a result, the corporate portfolio
- Establishing a formal investment review process with required stakeholders to change project elections

The optimize phase is most successful if you leverage many of the foregoing ideas and methods. As previously mentioned, a single unified CPM framework to make all investment decisions smacks of a portfolio cure-all, which is simply not practicable. Instead, develop tools and practices that serve as portfolio analytical tools. To understand what type of metric, framework, or investment funding mechanism to utilize, consult the following section on methods to optimize resource allocation, where tools such as Monte Carlo simulation, stage gating, real options, and others are discussed.

With regard to a formal investment review process, this can be done only when the data that is being collected as part of CPM is reasonably credible. The focus of an investment review is getting necessary organizational members together to demonstrably reallocate dollars between investments, units, product groups, markets, and so on. The goals of any initial review should be modest, given that the target is less about dollars and more about changing organizational behavior and demonstrating the organization's commitment to CPM. Future investment reviews can focus on more significant resource reallocation.

Setting Up The Review   If your corporate portfolio is being evaluated at multiple times in the year, it may be beneficial to conduct your investment review at the beginning of the year before investment spending has begun in earnest. Some high-level steps to follow are as follows:

- **Understand the current portfolio.** Before you steer the first investment review, you must know where you stand and where you want to go. Doing this means understanding what the current portfolio looks like and determining what gaps or opportunities might exist from an enterprise perspective. Example issues and opportunities include the organization's

- ○ Not doing enough investment in disruptive innovation
- ○ Having too many investments with no returns
- ○ Demonstrating period over period growth in a particular investment category that is too steep or too little (i.e., our marketing investments are down year over year and this is counter to organizational desires and strategic plans)
- ○ Possessing an inappropriate risk profile (i.e., too many low- or high-risk investments)

After understanding the portfolio, your review becomes easier if you can identify one area of over-investment and/or under investment.

- **Define your aspirations.** Based on your understanding of the portfolio, define your intentions for the investment review. Again, set your sights on modest reallocation as you begin. Examples of goals include
  - ○ Increasing percentage of investment portfolio focused on innovative investments from 3% to 5%
  - ○ Decreasing percentage and number of non–return-generating investments from 10% to 7% and reallocating money to those with returns
  - ○ Increasing investments in marketing by $1 million and decreasing investments in technology by the same amount
  - ○ Ensuring that 10% of the overall portfolio is in high-risk investments to provide a balanced risk profile for the company's investment allocation

- **Syndicate aspirations with the CPM champion.** The first investment review can be a contentious event, because you are entering uncharted territory. As a result, ensuring that your champion is on board with the goals and process is important. If the directive for the investment review originates from the champion, this will ensure that there is immediate organizational alignment around this effort.

- **Educate the players in the process.** It is important to present the investment review process and goals to those who stand to lose and/or gain investment resources as part of the process. A fundamental precept of a successful investment review is that those who stand to gain or lose should have a "seat at the table." You will need to educate these stakeholders on the goals and benefits of the investment review and ensure they understand that the reallocations being done will require their involvement and input.

- **Develop a hypothesis.** When you conduct your first meeting with the investment review team, you should have a hypothesis about what type of reallocations should happen (e.g., fund x, y and z investments and cut investments A and B). Leaving your meeting open to discussion with no preset hypothesis will ensure you have lots of debate and discussion but little to no results. Going in with a hypothesis frames the discussion and gives everyone something to react to. It is likely not the final outcome, but it is a starting point.

- **Refine and resolve.** Spend the time with the various stakeholders to promote healthy debate and constructive conflict among the participants. The final recommendation may resemble the initial hypothesis, or it may be completely different, but as long as the aspirations originally set out are being achieved, this is fine. It is important to empower each of the various stakeholders so that the ultimate decision is a collective one. This assures you of their buy-in after the recommendations have been formally committed to.

- **Implement recommendations and advertise.** Be certain that investment owners are apprised of changes to their investments. Communicate outcomes from the meeting to the CPM champion as well. Ensure that you advertise the outcomes and the important role that each stakeholder played in this process. It is important to make it clear that this was a cooperative process, one that benefited the entire organization.

- **Conduct the post-mortem.** Sit down with all involved to understand what went well during the investment review, what changes they would suggest for the process, and so on so that these can be integrated into any future investment reviews.

An excellent example of an investment review can be seen in the case of American Express.

Are We There Yet?

As you successfully navigate the four phases of establishing a CPM capability, enjoy the successes and accomplishments along the way. Most important, document the many benefits to your organization that CPM has enabled as these benefits will be myriad and deserve to be cataloged. Unfortunately, employing CPM is not a journey with an end point. CPM is a bit like the Greek myth of Tantalus, who was forced to "stand in a pool of water beneath a fruit tree with low branches. Whenever he reached for the fruit, the branches raised his intended meal from his grasp. Whenever he bent down to get a drink, the water receded before he could get any."[1] Your corporate portfolio can always be optimized further.

This may not be the sanguine result you were expecting, but this is the pragmatist's view of CPM. The first time through the four phases is undoubtedly the hardest effort related to building a CPM capability, and consequently the accomplishment is a significant one. But to ensure that the capability you have worked so hard to realize continues to remain relevant, it is important that CPM continue to be propelled forward. And this means "starting over" and analyzing how things are done with an eye to reengineering and reinventing your CPM discipline. Many times, this may represent a great opportunity for you as a CPM leader to move onto another role and bring in a new perspective to further refine CPM. This constant refreshing of your CPM capability and the talent surrounding it will ensure that it continues to progress and sustain itself within the organization.

TECHNIQUES AND TOOLS TO OPTIMIZE YOUR CORPORATE PORTFOLIO

Avoid one-size-fits-all metrics and resource allocation frameworks because while they can serve as useful diagnostics in your evaluation of investments or your portfolio, they cannot determine how your organization should be managed. No metric or framework is infallible. They are conversation starters and ways to screen investments or the portfolio, but blindly following these will lead you down a perilous path, where your own credibility and that of the CPM discipline will be questioned.

The alternative in this case is to think thoroughly about which metrics, tools, and frameworks should be employed to enable better investment and portfolio decision making. The following discussion provides an adaptation of a framework that was developed by the Working Council for Chief Information Officers. It basically offers the logical premise that as you spend more on an investment and as the complexity and/or variability of investments goes up, the complexity of the evaluation frameworks or tools you utilize must also go up. The methods given in the framework by no stretch of the imagination capture all the possible methods out there, but they have been selected for their unique approach to investment decision making and to demonstrate the diversity of techniques available to you to improve your organization's investments and performance. Some are highly quantitative and others are processes that can be utilized to improve investment decisions and performance. Refer to Exhibit 2.5 for an example.

ROI and Payback Period

ROI is usually defined as the sum of all cash inflows divided by the sum of all costs during the life of a project. ROI is the metric of choice when evaluating investments and is often talked about as an aspiration when it comes to measuring marketing or IT investments. Part of its allure is its simplicity in that it seemingly gives you the single most important piece of informa-

EXHIBIT 2.5 EVALUATIONS FRAMEWORKS AND METRICS

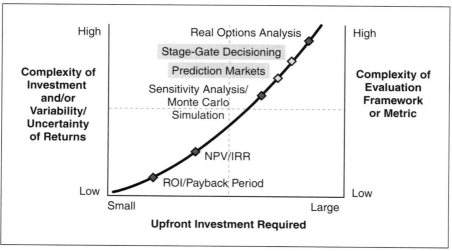

tion most decision-makers desire—what am I getting for the resources I am expending on this initiative. In fact, ROI is quite a solid metric to use for many types of investments, but it is most useful in investments where the variability and uncertainty of returns are low. Initiatives that your organization may have significant history and experience with and where returns are trackable, such as direct mail or coupons may be evaluated using ROI. Put all the investments in Excel, sort by ROI and draw a line where you have an expectation of an ROI minimum and select all those investments that meet or exceed the floor you have set, because the underlying ROI hypothesis is that investments that maximize ROI are what you select. Or you can start from the best ROI and choose all those investments as you go down the list until you have spent all your money. Using ROI is simple and can be effective in some instances.

ROI, however, is riddled with numerous problems that make it a flawed metric for all types of investment and portfolio decisions. These limitations and their consequences are shown in the following table.

Limitation of ROI	Consequences for Its Use
• Setting a high ROI hurdle rate accounts for cash flow risk much less effectively than discounting cash flows individually over multiple years.	• ROI is best suited to low-risk projects.
• ROI does not account for multiple possible outcomes or successive investment opportunities as a result of the project.	• ROI is a poor measure when investment may result in a wide array of outcomes or successive investment opportunities.
• ROI's utility decreases as forecast horizons extend and the time value of money becomes more critical.	• ROI is a weak valuation metric for long-lived investments.
• As a rate of return, ROI says nothing about the amount of money invested in the project.	• ROI is inadequate for comparing competing investment opportunities when amount invested is a deciding factor in resource allocation.

Source: Working Council research, 1997

Payback period is the amount of time cumulative investment cash inflows exceed cumulative project costs. Payback period as a criterion for investment evaluation is good as a measure of risk, but because it does not consider cash flows after the payback period nor does it consider when cash flows come in prior to payback, its applications and utility are limited. Additionally, determining what is a good or bad payback period is a bit arbitrary. While in a sense, it is a metric to capture risk, it does not explicitly consider risk within the cash flows that comprise it. Again, projects that are shorter term in nature and less volatile or less complex may be good candidates for using payback. It can be useful as a proxy for risk, but because it fails to consider the reward aspect of an investment, it should not be a metric used on its own for investment selection.

Net Present Value and Internal Rate of Return

Net present value (NPV) is defined as the sum of discounted cash inflows minus the sum of discounted project costs. This is a favorite of finance professionals, and, again, an Excel spreadsheet with investment NPVs can be sorted and all investments with an NPV greater than zero could be selected. NPV is good on many fronts as it does consider time value of money, it aims to consider project risk by discounting cash flows, and it is relatively easy to use. For investments for which risk can be approximated and where outyear cash flows are not highly uncertain, NPV is suitable.

However, the discount or hurdle rate to be used in an NPV calculation can significantly over or understate the NPV calculation based on how well or poorly it captures risk. Many times, organizations will adopt a single discount rate or several rates based on geography or products, but this does not consider the risk of the individual investment. Additionally, NPV is a single estimate of investment value when a range is usually more useful based on different scenarios or sensitivity analysis. Additionally, if your organization has several hundred or even thousand investments as part of CPM, changing the discount rate can have major implications from a process standpoint in order to make those changes in hundreds or thousands of Excel spreadsheets.

Internal Rate of Return (IRR) is the discount rate that equates cash inflows with cash outflows. Essentially, IRR is the rate that yields an NPV of zero. IRR is useful because it considers all cash flows as well as time value of money, and when utilized as an organizational hurdle rate, it is relatively easy to understand.

The issues with IRR include the fact that it is actually possible to have multiple IRRs. Additionally, IRR does not consider the size of investment in the initiative. IRR also does not tell you the dollar impact to the firm if the investment is actioned as it is expressed as percentage. Despite these limitations, IRR has uses in investment decision making. but using it for large investments with uncertain or complex returns is inadvisable, unless, of course, forecasted IRRs include a range or distribution of returns.

Sensitivity Analysis or Monte Carlo Simulation

As investment funding increases and the complexity/variability of returns inches up, tools such as sensitivity analysis and Monte Carlo simulation can be useful. Sensitivity analysis identifies investment-specific drivers of revenue and/or cost that have the greatest impact on other financial and operating metrics. For example, what would the economics of a particular Internet marketing investment look like if a response rate via the Internet increased or decreased by 10%? It provides a means to understand the investments' drivers and the sensitivity of results to changes in these drivers. It allows an initiative owner and those reviewing an investment for funding to attribute different levels of risk to investment outcomes in order to be comfortable with the ability of the investment to deliver according to its stated objectives.

The limitations of sensitivity analysis are mainly the time it takes to develop the scenarios and the involvement of others that is generally required to build robust analyses. Sensitivity analysis can be unwieldy; therefore, it is better suited to investments where funding is significant, because the time required to do a sensitivity analysis is warranted only for larger, more material investments.

Monte Carlo simulations and the Monte Carlo method (MC) are something that some may have intuitive familiarity with. MC is a method for iteratively evaluating what is called a deterministic model using a series of random numbers. In the parlance of this book, a deterministic model is another term for a driver-based model. And MC is useful when the model being used is complex, is nonlinear, or involves many uncertain drivers. The goal is to determine how random variation, uncertainty, or error drive the model. Simply stated, this means using randomly generated numbers within acceptable ranges to change the drivers of the model and see the predicted performance of the model. The outcomes of the model are represented as probability distributions and confidence intervals, and can help tell you with what level of confidence you can expect a certain outcome based on the changes in the drivers.

There are numerous computer programs on the market that can easily plug into Excel to help enable MC. While a couple of paragraphs on MC cannot serve to explain this fairly complex modeling technique, it should hopefully demonstrate the applicability of MC for complex, highly uncertain driver-based models. Although MC is a relatively easy concept to understand in theory, its statistical underpinnings and computational complexity can make it prohibitive to put into operation and difficult to understand; therefore, it should be used only on select investments whose returns are uncertain.

Prediction Markets

Prediction markets are a relatively new phenomenon within corporations but have seemingly caught on as a tool to help make better decisions by improving prediction capabilities. The likes of GE, Best Buy, Nokia, Samsung, Eli Lilly, HP, and Time Warner, to name a few, are using prediction markets in various capacities. The principle behind prediction markets is closely aligned to the concepts detailed in James Surowiecki's book *The Wisdom of Crowds*,[2] in which he argues that "large groups of people are smarter than an elite few, no matter how brilliant. These groups are better at solving problems, fostering innovation, coming to wise decisions, even predicting the future."[3] While Surowiecki's implications for prediction markets are far reaching in terms of impacts on economies and even on our daily lives, the concept has potentially powerful implications as applied in decision support tools for corporations, especially if they are building a CPM capability and evaluating large, highly uncertain projects.

Let us first understand how prediction markets work by taking an example in which a prediction needs to be made on projected sales for next quarter. Typically, the head of sales or a small team of management might make this prediction. With prediction markets, a competitive exchange or market is generally established where the entire sales team would make their prediction about the sales forecast. The market dynamic introduces an element of competition into the system, motivating people to participate, and with this increased input come better predictions about drivers. Prediction markets are said to be as good as or better than traditional prediction-making methods, and some vendors offering prediction market software claim their users have actually seen predictions 75% more accurate than those provided by the status quo.

With CPM, prediction markets can be used to help better predict investment drivers or results. In the case of a technology project or a new product launch, they can be used to predict whether the initiative will launch by a particular date. Prediction markets are a great way to engage employees and involve them in the creation of investment projections and drivers and ultimately to increasingly socialize CPM within the organization. Given the complexity of prediction markets and the cost of a system to enable this, these should only be used in larger projects where highly uncertain outcomes are anticipated.

Examples of corporate applications of prediction markets are provided in Exhibit 2.6.

Stage Gating

The tools and frameworks discussed so far help either in making better predictions or in the selection of investments from a potential list of opportunities. Stage gating is a powerful capability that can actually help an organization select the right investment upfront and then monitor a given investment on an ongoing basis to ensure that it remains an attractive opportunity. It is a widely accepted approach for managing large or multi-year investments through multiple review and decision points to examine progress against interim goals and then re-affirm funding.

In order to make CPM a funnel where investments actually get killed, stage gating is a powerful process and capability to employ. At the start of large multi-year projects, a detailed CBA is created before investment funding is granted. Along with this CBA, project owners describe project milestones they will reach at regular intervals (typically quarterly, semiannually, or annually). Then at these regular intervals, a stage gating review team, which is a cross-functional team of investment reviewers, sits down with project owners to understand progress against milestones and evaluate any required changes to the CBA. Based on the outcome of these discussions,

EXHIBIT 2.6   EXAMPLE OF CORPORATE APPLICATIONS OF PREDICTION MARKETS

Company	How Predictive Markets are Used	Results
General Electric	• Used to generate new ideas in Research Division • 150 researchers anonymously submitted ideas and each one was made into stock • Participants traded on viability of opportunity • Top performing ideas received funding	• More high quality ideas generated vs. status quo • Markets across GE businesses. Some as few as 25 traders with some having thousands. • Used for resource allocation, event forecasting, corporate governance and product development
Best Buy	• Used by 200 employees to predict sales figures, product launch dates	• Plan to rollout to all Best Buy employees by Q1'07
Samsung	• Used to forecast commodity prices within the computer industry for next 3 to 12 months	• Traders from Korea, US and Europe participate in the same market each bringing their local knowledge to the market trading

Source: Consensus Point

projects can be killed, given additional funding and resources, or put on a watch list for closer evaluation.

A typical stage gating process timeline is shown in Exhibit 2.7, but the number of gates required varies, based on the organization's desire to monitor and track investments and the nature of the investments.

The gates as discussed would look something like the example shown in Exhibit 2.8, which is focused on stage gating for technology investments.

EXHIBIT 2.7   STAGE GATING PROCESS FLOW

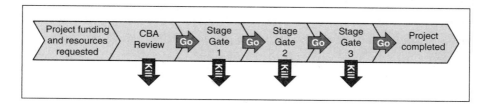

EXHIBIT 2.8   MAKING INVESTMENT DECISIONS USING STAGE GATING

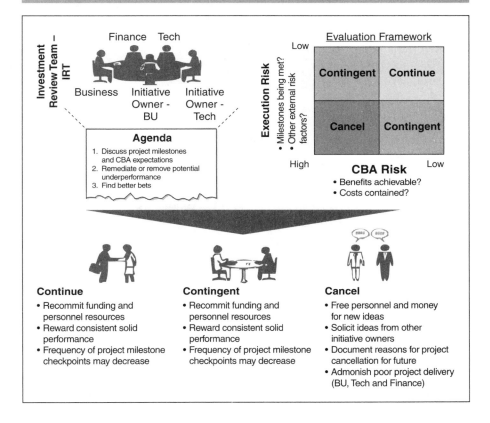

The aim of stage gating is to rehabilitate projects that have slipped, kill projects that are beyond saving, and reallocate funding to attractive unfunded opportunities.

Stage gating can require a seismic behavioral shift at companies because it does entail killing projects, which is not something all organizations are comfortable with. But if the mindset required for stage gating can be assimilated into the organization, it allows for better decisions to be made and for better investments to be selected. Additionally, stage gating rewards project owners who deliver results, and it holds those accountable who fail to deliver results. Exhibit 2.9 provides an example of a successful stage gating process.

EXHIBIT 2.9 COMPONENTS OF AN EFFECTIVE STAGE GATING PROCESS

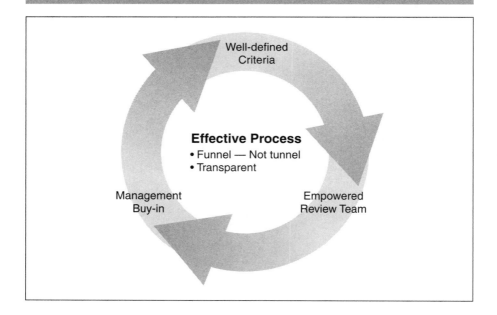

This process is seemingly intuitive, but many organizations that implement stage gates fail to think it through. Initiative owners must have a clear sense for how they are being evaluated, which requires having explicit go/no go criteria. Having a stage gate council or empowered review team whose recommendations will be heard and followed is obviously requisite to ensure that stage gating is credible and followed. Finally, management buy-in is essential. If an investment owner fails and, as a result, has investment funding taken away, the decision of the review team must stand. If the initiative owner can just go to senior management and secure the funding, the stage gating process becomes an ineffectual process.

Despite the myriad benefits of stage gating, it is not an easy process to implement and so is best left for large multi-year projects. It requires assembling a central review team, and it will likely require a team of people to monitor investments and evaluate CBAs on an ongoing basis. Because of the organizational resources required for effective stage gating, it should be approached and structured in a way that ensures that organizational value is maximized, given the investment required.

Real Options Analysis

Real options analysis leverages options math (i.e., Black–Scholes) as a tool to promote thinking about a range of options and to inform investment decisions. It enables analyzing a range of options on a variety of investments to determine which options are worth continuing and which should be dropped. The basic premise behind the analytical framework is to help keep options open and enable riskier options to be explored without making long-term commitments to them.

> "A real option exists if we have the right to take a decision at one or more points in the future (e.g., to invest or not to invest). Between now and the time of decision, market conditions will change unpredictably, making one or other of the available decisions better for us, and we will have the right to take whatever decision will suit us best at the time."[4]

Venture capitalists, economists, and others have long used real options to be a helpful tool in decision making. Recently, it has been extended to technology and research and development investments.

Its value in a CPM capacity is that real options force investment owners to determine whether the investment needs to be made now or whether it can be evaluated at some time in the future. This ability to free up funding in the near term is useful, because this funding can then be deployed to other initiatives.

The negatives of real options lie mainly in its complexity. Option math is complex, and its conceptual underpinnings may seem difficult to translate to a technology or research and development investment. Additionally, the value of a real option is severely impacted by the inputs used, and highly uncertain and flawed inputs can lead to erroneous predictions based on real options.

There are many books and publications that can walk a CPM practitioner through the technical underpinnings and applications of real options. For investments that are multi-year and highly risky, viewing them as a series of options has potentially powerful implications for the funding these initiatives receive.

Notes

1. Wikipedia, http://en.wikipedia.org/wiki/Tantalus.
2. *The Wisdom of Crowds*, Anchor Publishing, August 16, 2005
3. The Wisdom of Crowds, Inside Flap, James Surowiecki, Anchor Publishing, August 16, 2005
4. Colorado State University, http://dare.agsci.colostate.edu/csuagecon/extension/docs/agfinance/afr03-01.pdf.

CHAPTER 3

Applying CPM to Functional Areas within the Organization

You may not want to deploy corporate portfolio management (CPM) across your entire organization to start as there maybe specific functional areas of the organization where the principles of CPM can be applied initially to drive demonstrable impact. Starting CPM within one area of the organization may ultimately serve as a catalyst for other parts of the organization to move toward a CPM capability. Specific business units, product groups, or geographic markets may represent good starting grounds for CPM. Additionally, deploying CPM functionally—for example, across information technology (IT), innovation/research and development, marketing/advertising and promotion, capital planning or sales—may also represent fertile ground for CPM. Specifics on how CPM can be deployed across these functional areas are given in the following section.

INFORMATION TECHNOLOGY

IT has probably done the most to bring awareness of CPM as a discipline because IT continues to be "an enigma wrapped in a conundrum." Consequently, the industry that has emerged around CPM—or what is more commonly known as Project Portfolio Management (PPM)—has surfaced largely because of a focus on IT. Beyond the commercial ecosystem focused on CPM, which is a fairly recent phenomenon, numerous groups have been struggling with the question of making sense of IT for some time. MIT's

Center for Information Systems Research (CISR) which aims "to make sense of business IT" has been working on this issue since 1974 and readily acknowledges that this problem remains to be solved. Gartner, a prominent research outfit focused on technology-related issues, actually has found that two-thirds of technology investments do not achieve their intended benefits, demonstrating the difficulty in realizing IT value. So if some of the smartest people in the world, such as researchers at CISR and Gartner who have been working on the question of IT value for some time, cannot make sense of IT even with significant effort, resources, and information, how can a time-, cash- and resource-starved CIO, CTO, CFO, or senior technologies manager possibly do this?

The simple answer is that it is not easy. The IT landscape changes often. Every week, some industry pundit is lauding a new technology or practice as the next big thing. Organizationally, IT is generally focused on servicing the customers it has in the business while also ensuring that mission-critical systems continue to work without issue. These factors make the job of a CIO, CTO, or anyone focused on delivering IT projects quite difficult.

To make sense of IT, you need to avoid self-selection biases, which are highly prevalent in current work focused on IT value. Most of the consultants, experts, and think tanks working on the issue of IT business value begin by asking "What is the business value of IT?" The problem with this question is that it assumes that you are actually able to measure value. The plain truth is that most IT organizations cannot or do not do this. In fact, a recent global survey of 150 CIOs by Accenture found that while 75% of companies recognized the need for metrics tied to business goals, only one-third currently use them. Knowing is not doing; even though metrics are the rage, most IT organizations have not defined them. And, as the saying goes, "If it is not being measured, it is not being managed."

Given this deficiency, it is apparent that CPM represents a capability that can be used to define, track, and refine these metrics while making decisions about IT-related investments. CPM can also integrate with existing processes already in place within IT in the form of Program Management or Portfolio Management Offices (PMOs), architecture and security reviews, solutions delivery teams, and a host of other processes. In some instances, it may be worth rethinking some of these processes as they are generally very annual budget oriented (e.g., is your project over or under budget?). While this is important, there is a more important question, which is "Why are we doing this project in the first place?" A CPM capability is about enabling a discipline, but it has to be properly constructed; weighing it down with existing, ineffective processes does it a disservice. Once you have built a CPM capability within the IT organization, you will be able to answer and offer insights on the following questions:

- Is any individual IT investment proposal worth pursuing?

- Are our current practices for managing our IT investment portfolio adding value?

- Where are we investing our IT resources today, and what value is it bringing to the business?

- How do I communicate this value to my senior management and other stakeholders?

- Are IT, the business, and finance properly aligned when thinking about IT investments in a way that forces accountability and transparency?

IT investment evaluation using CPM means focusing on the upfront and ongoing rigor of these investments—and not just costs, but promised benefits as well. So it is important to ask several questions when an investment is just a proposal. The most important first element IT should aim to understand is "What is the business partner really asking for or in need of (e.g., what business problem are they trying to solve)?" If the determination is that technology is not required, let the business partner know that you have a solution that does not involve technology. If, however, it is determined that technology will help solve the problem and that IT should be involved, the next step is going past rudimentary, superficial high-level estimations on strategic benefit or on risk and actually quantifying some of these impacts. Even if the projected results from a profit-and-loss perspective do not accrue to the IT organization (inasmuch as they probably go to the business), it is important to know whether the investment, in its totality, is a good one or not. This means that the model being used to evaluate the investment must be standardized and rigorous and must have standardized assumptions; in addition, it must also meticulously consider risk and align with business strategy.

It also means that the right metrics must be captured—metrics the business and others in the organization understand. Vulnerabilities over time, patches deployed, percentage of memory utilized, and so on mean little to most people in the organization, because they require interpolation to make the bottom-line impact clear. These IT metrics may be important for managing the investment, but there must be a translation factor of these metrics that the rest of the organization understands, and these business-friendly metrics must be in the models being used. If these factors are not being considered in current models, then the models used to value an IT investment must be rethought. If an initiative sponsor can just say the return on investment (ROI) of my investment is 150% with no support or an ad-hoc model, this practice must stop. By doing this, you can force upfront accountability on the part of the project owners—both IT and business.

From an organizational perspective, this accountability can be driven by having a credible "third party" to review these models once created. This group will ensure reasonability and completeness. Once you have gathered legitimate models of the various IT investments, you can then consider them as part of a portfolio where trade-offs can be made.

With the portfolio in hand, it is extremely important to track the progress of the entire portfolio and of individual investments over time, given that changes in the IT landscape as well as execution and CBA risks present significant challenges to these investments. Stage gating is a useful practice in this regard, because it enables you to determine whether the CBA initially created still holds or new execution risks threaten the project. For example, if an IT project was slated to cost $1M and generate $2M in profit and has run into cost overruns and is now going to cost $2M, that investment needs to be reevaluated. Or if an IT project that was initially going to deliver ten new applications within six months has failed and has delivered only five new applications, that project also should be reconsidered. There may be justifiable reasons for these overruns or delays, but it does not change the fact that the original aspirations for the investment have changed and as a result, it is no longer as attractive as initially thought and should be reevaluated. To this end, it is important that some projects get killed as a result of this process. CPM is a funnel, and not everyone or every project will fit through it. This may be a cultural shift for an IT organization or the business partners who make requests of IT, but this type of constructive conflict forces accountability and promotes responsible stewardship of resources. Also, it frees up resources from struggling or inadvisable projects for new initiatives. As a result, IT is delivering more business value per unit of investment. This can ultimately be translated back to customers and senior management and will result in the highly coveted "seat at the table" for IT.

This seat is not a birthright of an IT organization unfortunately, but it can be earned with the demonstration of value.

In many instances, demonstrating value for IT investments can prove to be tricky, given that they have no definable returns. It is important to push back on these investments as there needs to be some value that can be conveyed, even if that value cannot be translated into dollars and cents. It is possible for investment owners to hide behind claims of security or reliability (i.e., "if we do not do this, our data may be vulnerable"). This may seem hard to push back on, but it is important to ask (1) why has this been discovered now, (2) what about our current practices has resulted in this vulnerability, and (3) whether the investment could be delayed. It is easy for IT initiative owners to obfuscate the issues when talking to non-IT personnel, so you must insist that the reason be communicated in a manner that is readily understandable.

Once you have upfront and ongoing rigor, you have an investment portfolio that is believable. As an IT executive, you are in a strong position to say that you are driving business value. From a process standpoint, the ongoing rigor CPM requires forces IT, the business, and even finance to talk through an investment to ensure that they all consider it to be realistic. Not setting out realistic, achievable objectives ultimately means that the investment might be canceled down the road because of financial underperformance or because it has not made its milestones.

Demonstrating and delivering real value from IT is an imperative for a CIO or CTO, and, ultimately, CPM enables this. By helping to create a process that helps exhibit this value, it ultimately can make IT executives increasingly valuable partners within an organization.

INNOVATION/RESEARCH AND DEVELOPMENT

Today, imagination is probably the only means by which a company can gain an unfair advantage over its competition. This imagination is often manifested in the research and development (R&D) and innovation efforts that an organization undertakes. However, despite its vitality to long-term success, innovation is frequently the core function that is managed with the least consistency and discipline within an organization. The current "innovate or die" mantra espoused by many consultants and innovation experts raises awareness (along with panic) of the need for innovation but fails to acknowledge that innovation requires discipline and patience and can be expensive, especially if not approached prudently. Innovation cannot be exalted just for innovation's sake; instead, it must be tied to specific business goals and managed.

There are some organizations not moved by the panic as they feel they are doing enough innovation, and on the other side of the spectrum there are organizations that do not know where to start. Those that have bought into the panic and the new innovation credo and those who feel they are already doing enough generally have decked resources (internal strategy, scientists, engineers, management consultants, etc.) against these innovation efforts. For those doing something in the innovation arena, many, given the metrics craze, are trying to put metrics around their innovation process by measuring such things as the size of their R&D budgets, the number of patents filed, the number of opportunities killed, and other metrics that "imply" R&D success. You will find ample evidence of these metrics being used to describe corporate and even national competitiveness, and what is most troubling about this is not the idea of using metrics to measure innovation but that the metrics being selected are not really indicators of innovation. They may be loose indicators of innovation activity, but as has been said, "never mistake activity for progress." The size of one's R&D budget tells you nothing about the efficiency or effectiveness of that expenditure. The number of patents filed does not tell you how useful those patents are, and in today's world, intellectual property rights are a lot less meaningful unless you are willing to aggressively and proactively protect them. The number of opportunities killed is a metric that tells you nothing about the quality of the ideas coming through your pipeline, and if you are killing too many ideas, it may indicate that you are being excessively austere regarding opportunities where uncertainty reigns.

The metrics, even if we could agree on what the right ones are, are useful only if you have a process to encourage and manage innovation, because innovation is tough work. *Harvard Business Review* editor Nicholas Carr correctly asserts "Innovation isn't free . . . innovation is actually quite expensive and quite risky."[1]

You cannot merely throw money at innovation as (1) you will not have enough money to address all the myriad opportunities that lie before you; (2) if you tried to chase every opportunity, you would end up with nothing; and (3) merely throwing money at innovative ideas does not work. A December

2005 Bain study of the Global Innovation 1000 (the 1,000 publicly held companies from around the world that spent the most on R&D in 2004) found that throwing money at innovative opportunities does not ensure success. In fact, their study revealed that "There is no relationship between R&D spending and the primary measures of economic or corporate success, such as growth, enterprise profitability, and shareholder return." At the same time, the study found that spending too little on innovative opportunities can actually hurt. In essence, the Bain study revealed that you should not spend too much or too little—not a particularly profound conclusion, but one that underscores the need to pick your opportunities and spend efficiently. Their study goes on to highlight that superior results, in most cases, seem to be a function of the quality of an organization's innovation process (i.e., the bets it makes and how it pursues them).

"At the spending levels represented by the Global Innovation 1000, companies can maximize their return on innovation investment through better processes for ideation, project selection, development, and commercialization. The imperative, then, is to identify the priority areas where process improvements will raise the curve the most," according to the Bain study.

For organizations that are trying to innovate, CPM applied to the innovation and R&D areas within your organization provides several benefits, as follow:

- **Visibility.** Most obviously, CPM provides a means to understand how much, if any, real innovation you are doing because it offers a portfolio view of where you are investing. If done right, it should also tell you what categories of innovation you are investing in and how much (e.g., incremental versus disruptive innovation). More than these high-level types of innovations, CPM can also tell you what subcategory of innovation you are undertaking—marketing, product, or process innovations. Many times, we make product or service development synonymous with innovation, but in actuality, there are many small innovations an organization can enable to give it long-term sustainable advantage. Toyota is a clear and amazing example of this. It is a generally conservative company that is always looking for ways to innovate its business processes. Over time, this has resulted in Toyota's gaining market share and boosting its valuation, stock price, price/earnings ratio (P/E), and so on. The visibility into the mix of innovation is very useful, because if you are really managing your business as a portfolio of opportunities; you want a mix of short- versus long-term bets, risky versus non-risky options, and so forth.

- **Speed.** The visibility that CPM affords you allows you to push initiative leaders to make a decision and move more quickly. If you see something languishing in the idea stage for too long, you can get on the phone and call that owner and ask why things have not progressed. CPM enables an organization to hold people accountable for a lack of progress and reward those who are making things happen. Shorter product life cycles, the emergence of technology, and a flatter world all conspire to make moving quickly more important, and CPM provides you with information to push the pace and keep up.

- **Reality.** Many times, organizations and their members feel they are being innovative, but after looking at CPM data, it becomes apparent that they are mistaking incremental "flavor" innovation for real innovation. By flavor innovation, I am talking about the relatively simple more chips in the cookie, added features in the car, new color of the credit card, or typeface innovation. While these changes can and should be made to respond to customer needs, keep up with competitors, and optimize the existing business, advantages due to "flavor" innovation are not generally long lived. Companies need to have a real sense for whether they are good or bad at disruptive innovation, because if they are not doing it, they can be sure that a competitor or upstart is going to do it to them.

- **Measurability.** One of the main things research on innovation reveals is that it is better to kill fast and often so that you can pursue many opportunities concurrently and quickly move toward those that show the most progress and promise. CPM enables you to see when an idea originated, how quickly it is moving through the pipeline, and whether sufficient progress is being made vis-à-vis this idea. A stage gating discipline that can be integrated with CPM can also offer significant benefits when trying to track investments. Measurability is particularly helpful for companies that believe that they can throw lots of money at a couple of opportunities and then build a product or service that will become the new "category killer." Emboldened by the likes of Apple and Google, many companies think that creating the next big disruption can be achieved by throwing money and resources at an opportunity. CPM can, if allowed, let you invest lesser amounts in each disruptive potential opportunity while investing more across many opportunities. It will invariably kill some of the sexy ideas that exist, but this is healthy because the resources saved can be redeployed to more promising ideas.

Here are a few cautionary notes when using CPM to manage your innovation and R&D efforts.

- **You still have to come up with the ideas.** Innovative ideas are not going to emerge from a CPM discipline. The ideas may be more appropriately or quickly moved through the pipeline, but the ideas need to come from you and other inspired creative people within your organization.

- **Ask for the right metrics.** Although I have advocated data-driven decisions throughout this book, innovation is the one category where I believe intuition can and must dominate. This does not mean rigorous analytical, data-driven decision making does not have a place, but rigor can be sacrificed to ensure that ideas are being encouraged and generated. Subjecting an innovative opportunity to the same CBA treatment is wrong, because an investment that an organization has done tens or hundreds of times has a great deal more data than an innovative opportunity. Creating rigorous driver-based models for innovative opportunities where you mathematically determine that your organization will one day own 2% of a trillion dollar market and this will generate $X billion of net present value is a colossal waste of time.

  Instead of sinking efforts into developing driver-based models for opportunities that may not even be realized for several years, it is more important to focus in on several more salient data points and questions. Many of these have answers that are extremely qualitative and that should be considered as part of your CPM discipline.

  ○ Is the market opportunity and demand sufficiently large to warrant investment of organizational resources and time?

  ○ What competencies and assets do we bring to the table that give us advantage as we enter this area?

○ Who are existing competitors, and what is the current competitive intensity?

○ What are the execution, operational, and exogenous risk factors that should be considered?

○ What is our plan of attack (i.e., what milestones do we expect we will be able to reach and over what period) to make this potential a reality and at what cost?

As you can see, the use of a CPM discipline vis-à-vis innovation is one in which much higher-level metrics and milestones are captured. These pieces of data and milestones should be vetted to ensure they are complete and logical and ultimately sufficiently interesting for the organization to want to pursue an idea.

It is important that the same pieces of information be collected across all such innovative opportunities to ultimately determine where resources should go. The one advantage of utilizing CPM for innovative opportunities is that the tracking of such opportunities is generally easier in the early stages.

- **Compare against similar investments.** If you compare an innovative opportunity against a business as usual investment when evaluating risk, financials, and strategic returns, this is an apples versus oranges comparison. You want to have both types of investments within your portfolio, but comparing two very dissimilar investments directly against each other generally will result in the selection of investments on improper grounds.

- **CPM will not solve for improper incentives.** If your organization has not moved up sufficiently on the behavioral front, CPM can help but will not compensate for the fact that if striving for innovation is not part of an organization's mission/DNA and rewards, ideas may be killed too quickly. Innovation does not always fall cleanly into an existing unit and does not fit with a risk-averse culture that is not comfortable with creating riskier but potentially valuable sources of future growth. If everyone in your organization is tasked on return on equity (ROE), ROI, IRR, NPV, etc and that is their decision-making frame of reference, innovation becomes difficult.

- **Keep resources for innovation.** When organizations face pressures on their business, they often look at the riskier investments and cut those first in an effort to focus on investments that provide returns today and that may help get them through the current rough patch. The perversity of this situation is that when things are good, companies are lulled into a sense of complacency and fail to invest in innovation because they assume the tide will continue to rise. For long-term success, this paradoxical cycle is a kiss of death. In bad times, try to keep your innovative investment funding pool or investments outside the purview of such cuts to ensure you are building for the future. In good times, be smart enough to realize that this will not go on forever and that innovation will be requisite to get you out of the inevitable adversity which is coming.

For organizations that do not know where to start with regard to innovation or do not see the need for it, there are probably more insidious cultural and political elements at play. Ultimately, if you are not innovating to position yourself for growth, you probably should be readying yourself for the sale of your organization or its long-term decline as others around you do change. If your organization is in this category, a forward-thinking executive can use CPM to begin cataloging the innovation the company is doing; in the long run, this data can be used to help make the case for doing more innovation. But be forewarned; moving an organization with this mindset can be a slow and laborious process.

Marketing/Advertising and Promotion

During the past several years, marketers have been challenged with the prospect of quantifying the impact of their efforts with a push to evaluate marketing as more of a science than as an imprecise art. CEOs and CFOs driven by shareholder value are increasingly interested in the ROI of their marketing investments, and a host of efforts have sprung up with the objective of helping to answer these questions. Many of these quantification efforts are dubious at best in terms of their validity (complex and unwieldy mathematical regressions and computer models that do not provide results that people can understand and believe), and more disconcerting is the fact that they are backward looking—they merely let you look at what you have already done with the aim of determining whether it was effective or not. This is a little too late in that the money and time have already been spent.

Yes, it is useful to know how you performed to hold people accountable, make changes going forward, and so forth, but it still does not inform or change the fact that the resources have been expended and could have potentially been spent in a better way. Additionally, this does not necessarily provide a means to project returns going forward, which is what is important. Driving while looking only in the rearview mirror is highly inadvisable.

These forward-looking efforts are not as prevalent as one would imagine given the huge amount of money being spent on marketing. Plain and simple, marketing is a big deal. In the first half of 2006, U.S. media spending totaled $72.98 billion, according to *Advertising Age*.[2] That is during only half a year.

Beyond the industry diversity, there are numerous marketing channels that are employed as given by *Advertising Age*. Note that because they do not include below-the-line marketing such as direct mail, total marketing spend is much greater.

Given all the channels available to marketers, a CPM capability enables you to know where you spend your money and to chart the course ahead. The idea of quantifying the value of marketing is one that CPM will not solve. It will, however, offer insights on how you can efficiently spend money to sell more and increase revenues, profits, and shareholder value.

For the sake of discussion, marketing will be categorized into three classes based on the exactness with which these types of marketing campaigns can be valued.

1. **Precise.** Consumer packaged goods and direct marketing firms are blessed with a wealth of information about their marketing investments As a result, with some amount of accuracy, these marketers can determine the effectiveness of their marketing campaigns. The impacts of a customer acquisition direct mail campaign, a coupon, a Google AdWords ad, telemarketing effort, Internet banner ad, and so forth can be easily discerned with available tracking capabilities. Failing to track these investments to see what works and to inform your future projections is a relatively easy gap to fix and should be done if it is not currently being done. An investment CBA for a data-rich initiative that details profit and loss benefits (revenues and operating metrics) and expenses should be created before any such initiative is begun. With the inventory of initiatives as part of CPM, you can then

make trade-offs between these investments to choose the ones that generate the best returns.

2. **Vague.** These are loyalty investments that focus on retention and changing customer behavior. While customer metrics such as sales, units sold, and so on can be tracked, it is generally difficult to discern how much of these metrics are attributable to loyalty investments. In the past, companies would use anecdotal evidence or loose extrapolations to gauge the effectiveness of these investments (i.e., our weekend sale generated a 25% lift in sales). Many organizations also use test and control cells to determine the impact of such investments. Ultimately this data can be used to project the returns for future vague investments resulting in CBAs and to allow trade-off decisions to be made.

3. **Uncertain.** This is where much of the big-ticket media spending falls. Although companies spend billions in this category and track marketing metrics with terms such as brand equity, consumer awareness, and share of voice, they have been unable to translate or demonstrate what a percent lift in any of these metrics translates into things that companies care about vis-á-vis revenues and profits. Creating a CBA for these types of highly uncertain investments is almost impossible. As a result, many marketing executives take a machine-gun approach to these uncertain investments by shooting many shots in the hope that something will hit. But with an organization pushing for metrics in other areas, it is incumbent on marketing leaders to try to take more of a sniper approach to selecting these investments, because not doing so puts their investments at a disadvantage. In tough times, it is these investments that get the axe because their lack of defined value makes them easy targets for cuts.

Just imagine trying to quantify the benefit of people seeing Geico's Gecko or Aflac's Duck or KFC's Colonel Sanders on their television screens? Yes— it is very difficult indeed. And given this difficulty, brand media budgets are often set using a lemmings-esque proposition of "let us look at our budget last year and see what our competitors are doing and follow their lead." For example, company BrandLoco (fictional) justifies its budget request by saying "Our competitor's advertising budgets are going up on average 8% year over year, so we should also raise ours by at least that much so that we do not lose our share of customer mindshare." (or any other preferred brand/ media metric). Conversely, if the advertising team at BrandLoco heard that their peers' budgets were going down, the response might be "This represents an opportunity for us to take share away from them if we fortify our brand media efforts right now." Both of these methods seem wholly imprecise, given the amount of media and advertising spend we are talking about (billions within a single organization at times).

Using CPM lets you understand how much of your organization's marketing spend is distributed across precise, vague, and uncertain marketing initiatives. It will also allow you to see what channels are being employed within each of these categories. And since you are viewing your marketing spend as a portfolio of investments, it is much more defensible when you have investments that have returns and others that do not, given that the total value of the marketing portfolio can also be provided. With the additional rigor that CPM provides, advertising executives and managers have better information to make decisions and to introduce an element of competition for marketing resources. Ultimately, this data-driven rigor can be used to convey the rationale for marketing's decisions to other key constituents in the company (e.g., CEO, CFO, business unit leaders, etc.). Additionally, over time, as the marketing organization gets more sophisticated about valuing investments, more of this information can be included in CPM.

It is also important to keep in mind that CPM should not be utilized to make marketing a cold, scientific exercise from which the art has been squeezed out. That would be unfair and inadvisable as well as highly disruptive to your marketing organization. Creativity and imagination are vital to marketing. Rather, CPM's goal is to bring measurable data to areas that historically were rarely measured. Within the marketing discipline, the beauty of CPM is that it can be leveraged across all marketing channels, making it a highly adaptable capability for marketing executives and the entire organization.

CAPITAL BUDGETING AND CAPITAL EXPENDITURE

Large capital projects remain a source of challenge for most organizations despite the widespread efforts and attention given to these projects. Research reveals that a significant number of executives deem the process as ineffective as a result of gamesmanship, politics, and conflicting views on organizational priorities. The ultimate outcome of this ineffective process is suboptimal funding to projects that are not worthy of investment.

So what is specifically driving these poor results in capital budgeting? A CFO Executive Board research survey revealed that one of the root causes of this failure is politicized decision making, which results in 40% of incremental expansions and 90% of discontinuous innovations failing to reach their growth and profitability targets. (See Exhibit 3.1.)

The CFO Executive Board study goes on to reveal that high project level failure rates are further magnified by the misallocation of resources at the initiative level, which ultimately causes overinvestment in smaller, incremental projects and less focus on riskier growth and innovation investments. To combat this issue, CFOs at certain prominent organizations, including Alcoa, Eastman Chemical, and Schlumberger Limited, keep an eye on the amount of investment going to "big bets." Per the CFO Executive Board, these companies "ensure that growth projects are not crowded out of the portfolio."

Let us take the example of Alcoa as chronicled by the CFO Executive Board. It became apparent that the company's capital expenditures were growing, but resources allocated to growth investments were falling,

EXHIBIT 3.1   **CAPITAL BUDGETING PROCESS ISSUES TODAY**

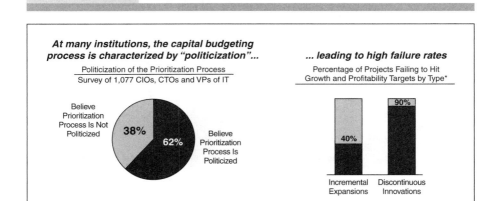

Source: CFO Executive Board, *"Disciplined Capital Budgeting Aligning Investment Proposals with Enterprise Strategy,"* July 2004.

EXHIBIT 3.2 ALCOA'S STRETCH FOR GROWTH

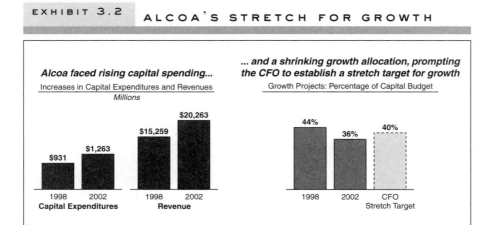

Source: CFO Executive Board, "Alcoa's Growth Spending Set-Asides," September 2006.

prompting the CFO to set a stretch goal for growth–oriented investments as shown in Exhibit 3.2.

As a result of the focus on the growth portion of its capital expenditure portfolio, Alcoa soon saw results, as indicated in Exhibit 3.3.

Pharmaceutical company AstraZeneca faced a different issue, also chronicled by the CFO Executive Board. Given the complexity of its many busi-

EXHIBIT 3.3 ALCOA MOVES ITS CAPITAL ENVIRONMENT FOCUSED ON GROWTH

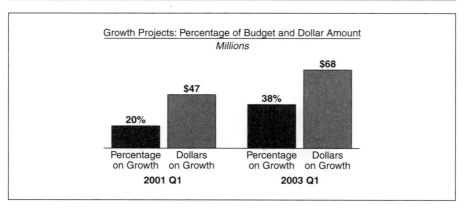

Source: CFO Executive Board, "Alcoa's Growth Spending Set-Asides," September 2006.

ness lines, the company needed a good way to prioritize among the myriad capital investment opportunities it had before it. The company used a portfolio approach to help make trade-offs between the various opportunities. (See Exhibit 3.4.)

John Patterson, Executive Vice President Product Strategy and Licensing at AstraZeneca, conveyed his belief in this portfolio management approach. "To be a successful pharmaceutical company, you need good products,

---

EXHIBIT 3.4   ASTRAZENECA'S PORTFOLIO ANALYSIS TOOL

Using an interactive tool, the Portfolio Management Committee can view the impact of alternative prioritization decisions on the portfolio...

Portfolio Analysis Tool
Illustrative

The committee can immediately see the portfolio impact of altering the funding priorities...

Sales   Value   Cost

Proposed Project Portfolio Choices

Priority	Therapeutic Area					
	CI	CV	Oncology	Respir- atory	CHS/ Pain	Infection
1	Project A	Project B Project C		Project L		Project 5
2	Project H Project J Project W	Project P	Project Q Project R	Project F Project I	Project N	Project 6
3	Project Z					
4				Project T		

... which allows it to perform "what-if" scenarios before committing resources

Source: CFO Executive Board, "AstraZeneca's Cross-Portfolio Prioritization," April 2006.

good ideas, and the ability to understand the financial implications of your actions. The key is to balance technical and commercial aspirations—balance enthusiasm with financial realities. A company can, through effective portfolio management, deliver top- and bottom-line priorities."

Given the problems seen in capital planning and budgeting and the results that a portfolio management approach can offer, the benefits that CPM can offer should be fairly obvious. CPM enables all investments to be considered side by side and removes some of the political, decibel-driven decision making that plagues capital investments. Instead, CPM replaces them with a data-driven portfolio approach that allows organizations to ensure that the appropriate amount of investment in risky and growth-oriented investments is being made. Because capital investments require more significant funding levels and typically happen over multiple years, CPM coupled with a stage gating discipline represents a powerful combination to improve capital investment decision making.

Sales Force

In talking to organizations with sales forces, they often respond by saying, "Why use CPM as we have customer relationship management (CRM) software that helps us manage our sales force's efforts?." Two incorrect assertions are inherent in this comment: (1) CPM and CRM are not mutually exclusive, in that the data contained in CRM can be used to help with a CPM capability and (2) CRM tools do not generally tell you the value of customers you are pursuing and those you have captured, but they do tell you who and what you are pursuing. This is the classic "measuring of activity" trap. Results do not count activity, and CPM is about understanding potential value and tracking sales-force–driven value.

CPM would enable you to determine what opportunities your sales force has before them and also to determine whether they are sufficient in value. If the value of these leads is not sufficient, you can redirect your salespeople to other activities or hold them more accountable for pursuing leads that are not sufficiently valuable to the organization. It may also signal to you whether incentives you have put into place are driving the behavior you would like to promote. Over time, it can be used to determine whether a salesperson or salespeople are delivering commensurate value with the resources being expended on them. More generally, CPM can help you determine whether building up your sales organization with new salespeople would be beneficial.

Notes

1. Wall Street Journal online, September 18, 2006
2. http://www.netscape.com/viewstory/2006/10/17/ad-age-top-200-brands-no1-brand spends-almost-1-billion/?url=http%3A%2F%2Fwww.metrics2.com%2Fblog%2F2006 %2F10%2F17%2Fad_age_top_200_brands_no1_brand_spends_almost_1_bi.html&frame =true

CHAPTER 4

Case Studies

Ⅰ am incredibly indebted to the many practitioners who spent time with me to share their insights and who helped me understand their corporate portfolio management (CPM) efforts. Their honesty in describing their successes, challenges, and even occasional failures has netted a very diverse and interesting array of CPM examples. From the list of organizations I have had the opportunity to chronicle, you can immediately see that CPM has applications across all types of organizations, irrespective of industry, size, public or private, for profit or nonprofit, and so on. You will also see that all of these organizations are at very different levels of evolution as it relates to CPM and that they have all tackled it in different ways, encountering different challenges along the way. In fact, many refer to their practices by different names or, in the case of companies that have built into their organizational fiber, by no name at all. However, at the heart of all these practices is the view that the organization is a portfolio of actions and initiatives. Although the benefits are different in size and the scope each organization took for its CPM efforts varies, the underlying objectives are quite similar.

From a practitioner's standpoint, the people chronicled in these cases are the people who are out in front of this still relatively nascent space trying to make positive organizational change happen, often with only a very crude map of the obstacles they may encounter. Given these unknowns, these are the "movers and shakers" in the field of CPM, those who are not waiting to learn and replicate best practices from others. Instead, these people are developing CPM best practices that are moving their organizations ahead of others and that will serve as benchmarks for other organizations. Of course, they have encountered bumps and bruises along the way, but that is to be expected when embarking on a path others have not traveled before. It is my hope that these examples will educate and inspire you in your own CPM efforts. For those who are still considering CPM and have not already started, the examples should hopefully increase your resolve to make CPM a reality within your organization.

It should also become apparent that CPM can be deployed across industry and functional areas within an organization as well as at the total organization/enterprise level. Given the ability of CPM to be deployed in as large or small a way as you would like, there are myriad opportunities to test the power of the capability before you take it to the entire organization. The following table illustrates the applicability of CPM across industries and functional areas. As can be seen, most areas receive a check mark indicating they can leverage CPM to improve decision making around investments.

Application of CPM across Industries and Functional Areas

	Financial Services	Healthcare	Manufacturing	Auto	Communications/ Telecom	Retail	Public/ Government	Education
Enterprise/Total Company Optimization (CFO, Corp, Fin,)	✓	✓	✓	✓	✓	✓	✓	✓
IT (Technology) Optimization (CTO/CIO, CFO)	✓	✓	✓	✓	✓	✓	✓	✓
R&D Optimization (CTO/IO, Head of R&D, CFO)	✓	✓	✓	✓	✓	✓	✓	X
Marketing Optimization (CMO, CFO)	✓	✓	✓	✓	✓	✓	X	✓
Sales Force Optimization (CMO, CFO, Head of sales)	✓	✓	✓	✓	✓	✓	X	X

AMERICAN EXPRESS

Key Company Information[1]
Market capitalization: $70.9B
Stock price: $58.86
P/E (ttm): 20.79
PEG (5 year expected): 1.50
Revenue (ttm): $25.1B
Net Income (ttm): $3.6B
Employees: 65,800

Company Profile[2]

American Express Company, together with its subsidiaries, operates as a payments, network, and travel company worldwide. The company issues cards to consumers, small businesses, and corporations through its own global network, as well as by third-party banks and other institutions in about 120 countries. American Express offer individual consumer charge cards, revolving credit cards, and various cards co-branded with other corporations and institutions. In addition, American Express issues travelers checks; various prepaid products, including gift cards, gift cheques, dining cards; and various incentive prepaid products. American Express also provides expense management services to approximately 100,000 firms through its corporate card program, corporate purchasing solutions, and business travel services. Its travel services include travel reservation advice and booking transaction processing; travel expense management policy consultation; supplier negotiation and consultation; management information reporting, data analysis and benchmarking; and foreign exchange and international payment services. The company, through American Express Bank, offers various investment management, trust, estate planning, and banking services; saving and investment products; various correspondent banking products, including international payments processing, trade-related payments and financing, cash management, loans, extensions of credit, and investment products; in addition, it distributes mutual funds and provides treasury and capital market products. The company also publishes luxury lifestyle magazines; travel and business resources; various general-interest, cooking, wine, financial, and time-management books; and international magazine editions. American Express also operates various websites, such as travelandleisure.com, foodandwine.com, departures.com, tlgolf.com, tlfamily.com, and skyguide.net. American Express was founded in 1850 and is headquartered in New York City.

Background: How Did CPM Emerge?

In 2001, American Express CFO, Gary Crittenden, sat down with the senior managers from the international card business to review strategic plans and discretionary investment spending. The group showed Crittenden an analysis that drove the group to reallocate resources between various markets they were participating in. The method they used to make these decisions had been dubbed Investment Optimization (IO), an effort by the group to determine which markets fit their strategic and financial priorities the best and then allocate resources accordingly. The group had built a rudimentary but effective software program that captured the data in hundreds of cost/benefit analyses that the finance unit was putting together, which, in turn, enabled these investments to be compared against one another and reallocations to be made.

This discovery was the starting point for an aggressive and company-changing use of CPM. Crittenden realized the power of this IO discipline could be significant and contacted Vince Nerlino, who at that time served as senior vice president for corporate planning and analysis to discuss the need to bring IO to the entire organization and its potential impact on total company resource allocation. The international card group had showed the power of IO. Additionally, Crittenden had been asked many times by the company's CEO, Ken Chenault, about what the specific returns on the company's investments were. Could IO have implications for the rest of the company and also provide an answer to the question that Chenault and Crittenden had been pondering?

Complexity Breeds Necessity

To understand why Chenault asked the question about investment returns and why Crittenden felt American Express might need the IO discipline at the time, understanding the size and inherent complexity of the company is important. American Express is a global payments, network, and travel services company with more than 65,000 employees, conducting business in nearly 150 countries. At the time the IO initiative was adopted, the company also had a financial advisory unit, American Express Financial Advisors (AEFA), which has subsequently been spun off. The sheer scale of the company in terms of the geographies it services, the varying levels of evolution and sophistication within the markets and customers it services, and the number of its products and services, coupled with the ever-changing payments space, serve to make American Express a hugely complex ecosystem.

As with any ecosystem, rules and practices become part of how things are done, and unfortunately sometimes, in the case of large organizations like American Express, these codified business practices may work for a particular department but do not always serve the best interest of the entire organization. Silos cropped up as did what can be called incrementalism. Various business units or product groups took their investment budgets as a birthright. If a group had $100 in "discretionary" investment dollars last year and they grew their revenues by 10% this year, they would likely be looking at $110 this year. The extra $10 in this example could be put to more of the same types of investments (i.e., incrementally allocating more resources to functional areas without necessarily taking a hard look at whether putting more into what was known and comfortable was the right thing to do).

Additionally, business investment owners were treating resource allocation as a once-a-year exercise, but in reality, it needed to be something that was reexamined on a continuous basis to ensure that changes within the marketplace and company were being constantly evaluated and that investment expectations were modified as a result.

In light of these challenges, Crittenden saw the power of IO to help break down these silos and provide an objective means to allocate resources to the best initiatives in a more dynamic year-round process. He also saw this as a way to enhance the flexibility of the organization, which, after witnessing and feeling the impacts of such events as the Gulf War and 9/11, the company increasingly valued. What if there was a way to turn off certain investments when the environment required? Conversely, what if a comprehensive list of unfunded opportunities could be maintained that could be actioned if business fundamentals or the environment allowed for it? Crittenden realized that the potential opportunity and implications were vast. He gave Nerlino the audacious goal of bringing this way of thinking about investments to the entire company within a year. The idea was not to incrementally put their toes in the water and see how CPM could work. The international group had already proven the value of CPM. It was now time to make this a reality across the enterprise.

Turning Vision into Reality

With the senior-level sponsorship of IO coming from Crittenden, Nerlino appointed Joanne Leong of corporate planning and analysis (CP&A) to head up the IO initiative. The group continued to work with the international unit, which had developed the IO software tool, to learn what the unit had done and understand what needed to happen to get other business groups into the process. Leong's group also developed an investment decision making guide called "Six Steps to Better Decision Making," which served as the company's underlying principles for investments. This was an important first step in that it provided a valuable resource to business units that they could give to investment creators; it was also the first attempt at developing a uniform investment decision making process across the organization. A summary of the six steps detailed in the guide follows:

Step 1: State a compelling business case. This is the foundation for any investment proposal.

- At a strategic level, it explains how the investment leads to a competitive advantage in an attractive industry.
- At the tactical level, it is sufficiently detailed to provide a basis for the assumptions being used and for providing insights into the key risk factors.

Step 2: Use realistic assumptions. Assumptions must be supported by rigorous analysis that draws on experience, peer comparisons, market research, and/or test results. Assumptions generally used to evaluate an investment include

- Key business drivers (i.e., number of customers, attrition, revenue, etc.)

- Level and growth of business drivers (i.e., difference versus status quo, scenario analysis)
- Startup and ongoing costs as well as fixed expenses

Step 3: Build a sound driver-based model and projections.

Step 4: Apply consistent decision making criteria.

- Use financial criteria such as net present value (NPV), internal rate of return (IRR), return on investment (ROI), and so on, subject to sensitivity analysis.
- Use strategic criteria to evaluate how investments align with strategic priorities.
- Use risk criteria to stress-test validity of assumptions and outputs as well as evaluation of external risk factors that may impact realization of benefits.

Step 5: Secure appropriate approval.

- Investments should be reviewed by management and approval is required for new initiatives and changes to existing initiatives.
- Approval process should be multi-level and ideally cross functional to ensure ownership and requisite scrutiny of investments.

Step 6: Conduct thorough post-implementation review.

- Project owners should track and report ongoing project success and issues.
- For multi-year projects, reviews provide quantifiable interim decision checkpoints and allow one to take corrective actions or kill projects not performing as they should
- Document lessons learned and apply what is learned to future investment analysis.

Six Steps has consciously and sometimes unconsciously served as the basis for much of the evolution of IO inasmuch as it was the first time that several key tenets of IO were formalized, including

- The use of driver-based models
- The importance of tracking results
- Using tracked results to inform future-year investment analyses

Six Steps is refreshed annually and has proven to be extremely valuable to American Express as a training tool for those working with investments and for helping the units, product groups, and so forth to develop better investment proposals for their internal review. But Six Steps, while a useful tool for these individual units, did not address two major outstanding questions required for an enterprise IO discipline.

- How do you define what an investment is?
- How do you create support for IO among the units?

What Is an investment?

American Express has taken a decidedly expansive view of what an investment is by describing an investment as anything that is discretionary. Virtually anything in marketing, sales, operations, reengineering, IT, CapEx, R&D/innovation, and so on qualifies. CP&A essentially said that anything not required to "keep the lights on" would be considered discretionary. The big departure from other companies that was made by American Express was to consider a large portion of operating expenses as discretionary instead of business as usual. The company also did not set a dollar threshold for what is or is not an investment, because of the varying sizes of business units within the company. So for one unit, what might be a tiny expense could be a decent-sized investment for another unit. Materiality level determination was left to the units, providing them with significant leeway in this regard.

Generating Support for IO with the Business

Despite having significant senior-level championing of IO from Chenault and Crittenden, the CP&A group knew that a "Ken and Gary want this" rationale for IO would not engender goodwill with their business partners. More important, they wanted to ensure that what was being built was collectively beneficial for the units. To do this, CP&A had to understand what factors would cause resistance or hesitation from the units. They (the units) were not accustomed to having to provide investment decision-making rationales to corporate or to provide investment data at the level of granularity that corporate was now asking for. They wanted to understand several questions in this regard.

Dialog

> **Unit question:** What was submitting this amount of investment information going to help them do?
>
> **CP&A response:** Although IO was deemed a corporate imperative, this was not to be considered a corporate exercise. Each of the units and segments, which are comprised of several lines of business, products, geographic markets, and so forth, would stand to benefit from the improved resource allocation that IO would allow. Optimizing the portfolio of the enterprise was important but was best done if the individual units and segments that comprise the enterprise were also optimizing their portfolios.

At a tactical level, this might mean that a unit would receive 200 investment proposals and, based on their own strategic, financial, and risk assessments; that unit might pick the 100 investments considered to be best. These 100 would then be submitted at a segment level, where segment management along with the unit subject matter experts would determine whether all 100 investments from this unit should be funded or whether there might be some opportunities to reallocate money from this unit's 100 investments to another unit with more attractive opportunities that could not be funded due to lack of resources in that unit. So this unit might end up funding 95 investments due to reprioritizations to another unit within the segment. Conversely, this unit might have the more attractive opportunities and would as a result get incremental funding from another unit and ultimately end up with 105 investments.

This process underscored the need for the units and segments to take IO seriously because this was something that would prove useful to their own management efforts. More important, since the models and analysis were already being done, there was not much in the way of incremental work required to meet the corporate objective of understanding where resources were going across the company. It meant providing this information to another consumer of the information— corporate planning in this instance.

Ultimately, enterprise IO would be enabled by units performing IO on their own, then it being done at a segment level; finally, this would roll up into enterprise investment optimization. Leong points out that "After the spin-off of American Express Financial Advisors (now Ameriprise), the organization consolidated business units under existing business leaders. What this meant for IO was that there was a greater need to optimize across segments that now had three to four very different business units making them up. IO became the means to offer this capability and visibility into investments and for them to make segment trade off decisions."

These varying levels of optimization are reflected by the illustration in Exhibit 4.1.

Unit question: Was this another bureaucratic process of questionable value?

EXHIBIT 4.1   CPM IS LEVERAGED AT AMERICAN EXPRESS AT MULTIPLE ORGANIZATIONAL LEVELS

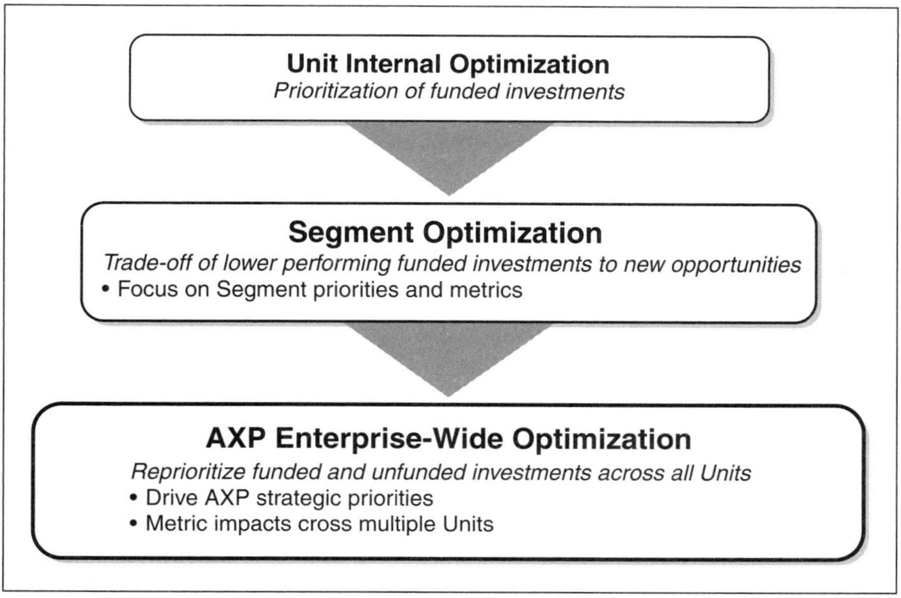

Unit Internal Optimization
Prioritization of funded investments

Segment Optimization
Trade-off of lower performing funded investments to new opportunities
• Focus on Segment priorities and metrics

AXP Enterprise-Wide Optimization
Reprioritize funded and unfunded investments across all Units
• Drive AXP strategic priorities
• Metric impacts cross multiple Units

CP&A response: Primarily, as detailed in the preceding text, the investment modeling needed to happen because solid business cases should be created irrespective of CP&A's involvement. Because the information was already being created, there was not a significant new workstream required. The work required was that the units and segments now had to submit their investment proposals to corporate, but since they had already created the investments, this was not a new, unwieldy process.

Beyond the efficiencies of the process, CP&A went out and sought to work with the units and segments to convince them that company IO was a useful discipline as "our paychecks all say American Express on them" and as a result, it is in our collective interest to ensure the company's resources are going to the initiatives that make our portfolio the strongest."

Unit question: Is corporate going to tell us how to model our investments?

CP&A response: The goal of IO is not to disintermediate the investment subject matter experts by creating some generic all-purpose investment model. Investment owners and creators should continue to model their investments as required in order to make effective decisions for their business. What corporate will aim to do is ensure that all investments do provide a base level of information to enable comparability across all investments, units, and so on. Accordingly, there are a set of corporate metrics that all investments should provide that are generally quite high-level in nature (i.e., revenue, expenses, NPV, IRR, pre-tax income, certain operating metrics, etc.). This does not mean that a unit that wants to model eight subcomponents of revenue should not do so. It should continue to model as required to make decisions, but for the purposes of total company investment reviews, there will be a smaller set of corporate metrics that need to be captured. One role that corporate also filled was bringing best practices to units by reviewing how different groups modeled their investments and then sharing the results of these "investment deep dives" with the units. This would result in changes to investment modeling as a result of the findings these deep dives uncovered. In addition, corporate would ensure that certain global assumptions such as discount rates, tax rates, foreign exchange rates, and so forth are centrally managed so that all units are using similar assumptions in these regards. Centralizing these assumptions ensures that investments from one unit to the next do not appear different simply because of the use of varying assumptions. Leong pointed out that this was one of the most significant ongoing challenges. "Even though we had initially gone through a level-setting process for valuation and calculating of NPVs and other metrics, there were still some variations in calculations for things such as fixed costs, equity cash flows, etc. that we continued to try to instill."

Unit question: How is corporate going to use this information?

CP&A response: IO is not a black box that will make investment decisions for the company based on some high-level corporate metrics and selection of the highest NPV or ROI investments. Again, the idea was not to disintermediate the units, who remain the subject-matter experts about their investments and business priorities. Additionally, IO was not going to zero-base all unit investment budgets. So, for example, if you had $100 last year to spend on various investment activities, you were not going to start with $0 this year and have to prove why you deserved money. Instead, IO would be used to evaluate those investments which can be considered "on the fringes"—those where the financial returns are low, risk is high, and/or strategic benefit appears minimal. The hope was that by looking at these "fringe" investments, the company could look to reevaluate and reallocate money between units and investments. It was also hoped that the greater transparency IO enabled would create internal competition for the best ideas, and this more meritocratic investment decision making favored those with great ideas and execution capabilities.

It was important throughout to ensure that the new units knew that this was not an adversarial relationship but one in which corporate and the units were essentially pulling in the same direction. In this case, corporate was just looking at things at a higher level and more holistically across the enterprise than the units would need to.

Making It Happen

In 2002, American Express, using the simple software tool that aggregated hundreds of Excel spreadsheets into a database, had its first corporationwide investment submission. The international unit continued to support the tool and help CP&A with many of the process elements. There were no major reallocations of dollars to start. The victory in this case was that this was the first time that the company had a snapshot of total company spending across business units, functional areas, markets, and product groups.

But reallocation was not something that was possible yet, because people were still getting used to doing IO, and despite some progress, there were still many questions circulating about the validity of the information contained within IO. Although significant progress had been made regarding standardization of corporate metrics and their calculations, there were still data issues. There were some outlandish NPVs and lots of investments tagged as strategic nonfinancial, which provided them a bit of a pass to submit expenses with no return information.

Despite the issues with investment modeling, it was still obvious that IO had started to creep into the consciousness of the company, with investment owners and senior management of the units increasingly talking about their IO plans. IO reviews within the units became more commonplace. One of the fundamental objectives of implementing IO—making resource allocation a hot-button topic—had begun to happen. But the data had to be fixed for reallocations to start happening.

The CP&A team, along with units that also started to see the benefits of IO, worked throughout 2003 and 2004 on getting the data picture cleaned up. As there were four IO submissions each year, there were several opportunities to analyze progress and hold those making investment projections accountable for progress on these data goals. In 2003, the team brought IO to the staff groups and utilities (shared service groups) because these groups also had discretionary investments they controlled that should be part of IO. By the end of 2004, the company had nearly 4,000 investment initiatives in IO per annum, aggregating to several billion dollars of investment, which represented 25 to 35% of the company's operating expenses. IO was by no means immaterial and the last 2.5 years had resulted in significant progress, but there was one huge area that had not been tackled.

Benefits Realization: Closing the Loop on Actual Results

In 2004 during an update about IO with Crittenden, questions about how actual results would be tracked came up, and it became apparent that there was no consistent, comprehensive process to enable comparison of promise versus performance (i.e., projections versus actuals). The first couple of years had yielded great work on the promise of IO, but in order for the company to realize the ideals it had laid out in Six Steps, benefits realization—the tracking of investments—had to become a reality.

Again, the company set an aggressive goal from the start, stating that investments needed to be tracked for three years. This, it was hoped, would be the means to ultimately "close the loop" on investments. Again, CP&A led the charge on rolling this out to the units. This time, however, the information available from an investment tracking perspective was quite disparate and nonuniform.

Some units had tracking systems that enabled investment-level tracking. Some units could track only at an aggregate level and others had very little tracking infrastructure or used offline spreadsheets to track results. Collecting this information would be much harder to do, given the diversity of sources for this information.

CP&A took a pragmatic approach to tracking, in that requiring every unit to track at the same level would not be practical, useful, or well received. So they let the units determine the level of tracking detail they would provide and set up two investment submissions per year to collect tracking information. Taking a heavy-handed approach with the units would have burdened them with significant work, because they already had 5000+ initiatives for each year. Tracking investments from two prior years meant that potentially 12,000+ investment initiatives would have to be evaluated at any moment in time. This is a massive undertaking that could significantly slow down the units if not constructed properly.

The goal of tracking was simple and echoed in Six Steps. American Express wanted to hold employees accountable for their results and create a continuous feedback loop that would improve future investment decisions. Exhibit 4.2 shows a high-level schematic of the process.

Let us take a simple hypothetical example for company Closed-Loop, Inc with 1,000 employees:

- An investment owner creates an information technology (IT) investment that calls for the purchase and modification of software to reduce calls to the IT helpdesk. The investment creator feels that this software will result in each employee's calling the helpdesk two times less per year than is typical. Because on average employees call the helpdesk four times per year, the owner feels that this initiative will result in a 50% reduction in helpdesk calls within six months. According to the investment creator, each call costs $10, so 2,000 fewer calls represents an ongoing benefit to the company of $20,000. Despite the aggressiveness of these projections, assume that the investment is approved and actioned.

- After the technology is implemented, investment results come in: from months 6 through 12, ClosedLoop, Inc actually sees a

EXHIBIT 4.2   HIGH-LEVEL INVESTMENT OPTIMIZATION PROCESS SCHEMATIC

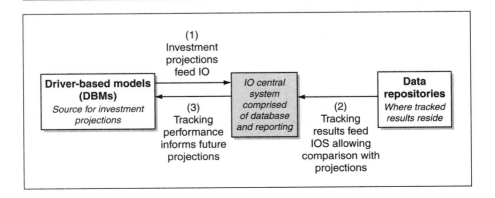

spike in helpdesk calls as employees who have not been trained on the new software are calling the helpdesk to understand what to do. After month 12, helpdesk calls do start to decrease but not by 50% as projected. Herein lies the first benefit of tracking—the investment owner and its approvers can be held accountable for their aggressive assumptions.

- In the following year, another investment is proposed that would move several Human Resources (HR) functions to a self-service Web application. Again, the main benefit of this Web tool is the lower number of calls that HR would get thereby reducing expenses and increasing productivity. Given the history that the company had with the helpdesk software, there is now the ability to examine this similar investment to ensure that some of the aggressive adoption assumptions as well as upfront issues are considered. Therefore, the overall investment costs and benefits should be more reasonable and accurate.

This simple example demonstrates the power of closing the loop that American Express was going after. While in this case, the accountability aspect was used to hold someone responsible for bad results, it can just as simply be used to reward and recognize those who are outperforming expectations. Closing of the loop as envisioned by American Express could and should be used for all types of investments (e.g., IT, marketing, operations, sales, etc.) and should serve as a means to institutionalize some of the knowledge about investment behavior that the company was seeing.

Making Cross-Segment Reallocation a Reality

By 2005, the company had made enough progress on data consistency and was on the road to closing the loop. For the first time, the idea of looking at the least attractive investments with the aim of tangibly reallocating dollars across business segments emerged, and in mid-2005, the company held its first investment review team (IRT) exercise in which this was attempted. As part of the IRT, each segment appointed a delegate who had a "seat at the table" and who would serve as the ambassador for the group as it related to any investment reallocations. Each unit was asked to put its bottom

10% of investments on the table and was also asked for a list of unfunded opportunities. The determination of bottom 10% was left to the units, but since corporate had all the same information, any "gaming of the system" could be largely kept in check by ensuring that the investments put up truly were, in some way, the worst investments.

As a result of the IRT, the company for the first time reallocated tens of millions of dollars between segments. The IRT succeeded because each of the units had a seat at the table, and so it proved to be a decision-making exercise that was not met with the expected derision. The company has subsequently conducted two more IRTs at the start and mid-point of 2006, which resulted in additional reallocations within and across business segments. Most important, the IRT represented a seismic shift in terms of organizational behavior for the organization with the reallocation of money.

Moving the Needle on Organizational Behavior

The deployment of IO was a "classic change management exercise," commented Alan Gallo, current senior vice president corporate planning and analysis. "Transitioning business leaders from a historical process where they were not being questioned to a process that now had transparency and competition can be difficult. The way the behavior change has happened was a result of two things: (1) sponsorship from the very top in our CEO as he had been asking for many years "'what am I getting for my investments"?' (2) the ability to get a couple of quick wins which we also had. And as a result, people gained confidence that we can do this."

Pat Burke, a business segment vice president of investment optimization in consumer, small-business and merchant services, (CSMS), echoed Gallo's comment that change management was key. This was made difficult at a segment level for many reasons, as detailed by Burke. "Historically before IO, the product and marketing organizations didn't utilize advice from finance either because they didn't want to or we [finance] just didn't give it to them. The product and marketing teams were used to getting what they got before, and there was not a lot of central oversight on individual investments. Things were ad hoc and nonstandardized, and additionally, there was little to no back end tracking."

Given these change management challenges, the IRT provided significant momentum for the IO effort and for changing organizational behavior. The success of the IRT was followed up with a first-time IO Summit. It is worth noting several key components of the IO summit, namely:

- The conference specifically called for people from the business to attend in order to provide them greater understanding of IO and its benefits.

- Senior-level sponsorship of IO was evident through participation by the CFO and other senior finance personnel.

- The resource allocation simulation conducted at the conference drove home the point that optimized portfolio resource allocation at a total segment or company level is improved when functional or business silos are removed.

- External speakers were brought in to provide a third-party perspective on various portfolio-management practices.

- Business units that had developed best-in-company practices regarding investment decision making were invited to speak in order to share their knowledge.

- An awards ceremony was used to recognize employees who had been instrumental in the deployment of IO across the company.

American Express's summit was another demonstration of the fact that the company realized that a process to enable IO was not by itself sufficient and that organizational behavior must also be modified to truly institutionalize IO.

Results and Accomplishments

Many accomplishments are probably evident for American Express's IO discipline, but the extent to which the IO discipline has impacted American Express in many facets is remarkable. Additionally, the various constituents involved with IO point to some of the same as well as several different benefits resulting from the company's efforts. Leong points out that through the company's efforts, "we've 'institutionalized' IO, and it is now a 'household name'. It is integrated into the way that the business makes decisions."

Most specifically, there were several tangible benefits at a business-unit level as detailed by Burke:

- "For our acquisition investments, we can prove returns have actually improved from '04 to "06.""
- "There is greater openness on the part of business partners to provide information and to look at IO. IO has become a synonym for investment analysis."
- "From a finance perspective, it gave us a seat at the table."
- "In the beginning, we relied on people having individual epiphanies and seeing the benefit of IO, but now it has become more universal."

From an enterprise perspective, Gallo, a 19-year veteran of American Express, points to several major benefits from IO:

- "If we look at the company's growth in cards over the last several years, IO has really helped in this regard. We've used a similar amount of resources to focus on the best investments, and as a result have been able to grow our cards by double digits."
- "The fact that there is a common language and there is a common denominator for measuring performance across the company such as ROI, NPV measures enables comparison across the company, and this is huge. Different functional areas are talking about IO. This common language is very important."
- "IO has actually helped us make some hard, but good decisions about getting out of certain businesses. In fact, when we spun-off AEFA, part of our rationale was that they [AEFA] would be increasingly competing for investment dollars with businesses that typically generate higher returns and that their investment funding could be limited in part because of our IO framework. In the pre-IO days, each business would get its allotment of resources."
- "The biggest behavioral difference is that businesses ask how the investments in other businesses are doing. Years ago, they'd never ask about that because we spread dollars around to make people happy. Now people question resource allocation decisions because there is a competitive internal market for

investment ideas. The dollars belong to the shareholder and now people have to compete for it. I've been here nineteen years and am seeing the difference."

Beyond these stated benefits, the following are accomplishments and results from IO at American Express from an adoption as well as a tangible benefit perspective.

ADOPTION HIGHLIGHTS

- All business units and shared service groups utilize IO for decision-making globally—nine business units, six shared service groups.

- All functional groups within American Express (i.e., marketing, IT, sales, R&D/innovation, reengineering, operations, etc.) are using the IO system/discipline to make decisions.

- Although it began as one, IO is no longer a finance exercise. Marketing people create their tactical marketing plans thinking of IO, and as a result, finance, marketing, risk all have a seat at the table and are involved with investment decision making.

- IO is utilized across more than 30 geographic markets.

- IO captures billions of dollars of American Express investment expense on a per annum basis representing approximately 25 to 35% of American Express's operating expense base.

- There are 5,000 to 8,000 unique investment initiatives in IO of all types on a per annum basis.

- Senior management talks about using IO to manage the business better, demonstrating that IO is becoming part of American Express's DNA.

TANGIBLE BENEFITS AND ACCOLADES

- The flexibility, improved decision making, and accountability IO enables has been cited by American Express's CEO and CFO within the company as well as in their conversations with Wall Street analysts.

- As a result of several IRTs, tens of millions of dollars have been reallocated within and across business segments, resulting in greater understanding of IO and a breaking down of organizational silos.

- Tens of millions of dollars of unfunded opportunities have been funded when additional investment capacity has existed or become available.
- Tracking of actuals completed for some units thereby enabling comparison of promise versus performance.
- The in-house–built IO solution was the winner of Baseline Magazine ROI awards for best new application and most innovative new application and was cited by Baseline as having a 2700+% ROI.
- American Express has been cited by many leading think tanks and has been the subject of seminars at many conferences on the subject of investment optimization and corporate portfolio management including CFO Executive Board, Gartner, Enterprise Portfolio Management Council, and the Beyond Budgeting Roundtable.

With this long set of achievements for American Express, it is also worth noting what has driven the success of IO at American Express. At its core, Gallo commented that "we are a data-driven company and culture which has helped this. Additionally, we have a CFO who has business experience, and he was clearly coming at this from a business perspective and not from a policing perspective. To run a business, he knew that we need to know the best places to invest our money. And we had a CEO that wanted to get the answers to the very specific question of how our investments were doing. The visibility of this as a goal has been significant. IO has been part of Gary's goals, and it links to compensation of his organization, which really has helped drive the momentum of this initiative on an ongoing basis."

Upcoming Challenges

Although American Express has made significant progress in its corporate portfolio management work, the company continues to try to reinvent and improve the discipline. Gallo comments that there is an "ongoing challenge year after year to keep the discipline in place. It is tempting for people to use lofty assumptions and so we need to hold people accountable. We need to continue the closing of the loop exercise so people can be informed from the past. And of course, finance needs to continue to promote the discipline."

Some of the specific challenges and development areas they are targeting include

- Developing methods that may help value investments whose returns are typically harder to monetize such as retention, advertising, technology, or compliance investments. Gallo feels strongly that "we need to get better at tracking the behavior of and results for investments which are not as easy to track, and we must commit to these goals."

- Further leveraging the IO discipline in conjunction with IT to provide additional rigor and evaluation of IT investments on an initial and ongoing basis.

- Utilizing more rigorous evaluation frameworks or tools when evaluating new or ongoing investments. Ideas in this arena include using predictive markets, real options analysis, stage gating, Monte Carlo simulations, and a host of other possibilities that the company hopes can be used by investment owners and those making decisions on investments so they can make better decisions.

- Further closing the loop and enabling more rigorous promise versus performance analysis to improve investment decision making.

TRANSUNION[3]

Key Players

- Cathy Madden, Vice President, Corporate Strategy
- Piyush Sanghani, Director, Portfolio Management

Key Company Information

- Privately-held company founded in 1968 based in Chicago, IL
- Employees: more than 4000 worldwide
- Provides solutions to more than 50,000 businesses worldwide
- Reaches consumers and businesses in more than 30 countries on six continents
- Maintains credit histories on more than 300 million consumers around the globe
- Market leader with leading U.S. businesses relying on TransUnion to interpret information, make better decisions, reduce risk, and improve opportunities. Leadership evidenced by customers, which include:
  - 48 of top 50 U.S. banks
  - Top 10 credit card issuers
  - 46 of top 50 auto finance companies
  - 9 of top 10 insurance companies
  - 17 of the top 25 collections companies
- Corporate structure:
  - Information services—Deliver solutions that leverage data, decision making technologies, and advanced analytics to help customers
  - International services—Facilitate the development and implementation of credit infrastructures around the globe
  - Real estate services—Enable mortgage lenders to manage and streamline the entire residential lending process
  - Consumer services—Empower consumers with the tools, resources, and education to better understand and manage their credit

Company Profile

TransUnion is a leading global information solutions company that customers trust as a business intelligence partner and commerce facilitator. TransUnion offers a broad range of financial services that enable customers to manage risk and capitalize on market opportunities. The company uses advanced technology coupled with extensive analytical capabilities to combat fraud and facilitate credit transactions between businesses and consumers across multiple markets.

TransUnion and CPM: Brief History and Highlights

Cathy Madden and Piyush Sanghani first learned of corporate portfolio management (CPM) at a portfolio-management conference. Although TransUnion had steadily grown throughout its history, they realized CPM would tremendously benefit the company because it was facing a number of challenges that many mid-size companies face, including

- A need to align decision making and improve communication across business units
- A desire to make smarter investment choices for only those initiatives that meet customer needs and drive profitability and growth
- A framework to establish a clear sense of ownership and accountability

Recognizing that TransUnion could greatly benefit from the application of CPM's philosophies, Madden and Sanghani were determined to implement it.

Because the company has several business units, Madden and Sanghani took a decidedly pragmatic approach to implementing CPM by focusing on a single department to get the process going. However, after 12 months of practicing CPM within the department, it became obvious that TransUnion needed to move beyond department-level prioritization to realize its full value. Undaunted, Madden and Sanghani went back to the drawing board and rethought CPM and how they could apply it to the company.

They decided to expand the scope of CPM to one of TransUnion's four major business units. Basically, it was time to tackle and take on what Sanghani calls the "800-pound gorilla," or TransUnion's main revenue generator, and apply it to other business units after a successful implementation. Fortunately, selling CPM to the business unit was relatively easy, because the department head that had previously championed CPM had been promoted to run TransUnion's U.S. business. Sanghani and Madden had successfully cleared two of the largest obstacles most other companies face when trying to apply CPM:

1. Securing a senior advocate and champion of portfolio management

2. Finding a business unit to pilot portfolio management and generating significant, favorable results that senior leadership would notice

By adopting CPM, TransUnion's business unit has evolved its discipline to think of its resource allocation in two ways. One way is portfolio management, which is defined as the process of actively evaluating, selecting, prioritizing, and monitoring investment opportunities to create optimal business value. The other way is called demand management, which is defined as a process that ensures that IT resources are allocated appropriately according to business needs.

Making Portfolio Management Happen at TransUnion

With a new "guinea pig" in place, TransUnion set out to apply CPM's philosophies again. First, they sought to clarify the definition of an investment. Sanghani said, "From our perspective, an investment could be just about anything including a product, acquisition, infrastructure or a new platform. At this point, we have a pretty broad investment definition, but we are working on determining where to draw the line." Although its definition is currently expansive, TransUnion has been careful not to bite off more than it can chew. Sanghani added, "We are currently focused on a mix of product and information technology investments. We began with product investments and expanded into information technology. Ultimately, we will look at business investments, but right now, we're focusing on the information technology expansion phase."

One parameter TransUnion has implemented involves the materiality level of investments, which has been set at anything requiring funding of $100,000 or more. "Although we have educated employees on portfolio management's benefits and most employees understand them, we have set up a system of checks and balances to ensure business unit leaders do not avoid the portfolio management reviews process by breaking up larger investments into smaller, sub-investments. We have established a series of processes within our finance, legal and project system so people can't circumvent the process," said Sanghani. "Although TransUnion takes only investments greater than $100,000 through this review, approval, and prioritization process, it reports on all projects that are part of the portfolio. This critical component provides TransUnion with a holistic view of where resources are allocated and how to best determine where resources may need to be shifted to maximize returns on the portfolio," continued Sanghani.

How Does TransUnion Evaluate Investments?

TransUnion has successfully standardized how investments are viewed and evaluated. Primarily, the company has standardized a cost/benefit analysis (CBA) process for all investments. As a result, the same metrics are captured for each investment even though the time horizon over which these benefits may be realized varies across investments.

TransUnion also developed a true portfolio view of investments, categorizing them into several large corporate imperatives: compliance/contractual, efficiency/effectiveness, growth, maintenance, mergers and acquisitions, and security. There are several subcategorizations that make up these larger classifications. The net result is that TransUnion has a unified view of all investments on a single dashboard.

To help in the evaluation of its many investments, TransUnion looks at discounted cash flow analysis, internal rate of return (IRR), earnings before interest and taxes (EBIT) as well as payback period. Sanghani said, "TransUnion also accounts for risk through the discounted cash flow expectations." Beyond the financial and risk elements, his group also ensures that the investments are aligned with strategic business priorities. It is a combination of "financial, other qualitative data and management gut feelings that help determine priorities," adds Sanghani.

Focus Areas for Portfolio Management at TransUnion Going Forward

Because the company has seen promise in how it has applied CPM to date, Sanghani and Madden continue aggressively to push to improve the organization's efforts. On risk assessments, Sanghani aims to "figure in other risks, such as market, execution, and technology to provide a more complete view of risk. We had a risk index at one point, but it was too subjective, so we're trying to make it more robust and scientific."

While the company has a good sense for where it wants to go, Sanghani acknowledges that "Portfolio Management and Demand Management are not completely in sync just yet. We would like to bridge the gap between CPM and Demand Management to eventually set priorities by taking resource availability into consideration."

The company continues aligning CPM with the financial planning, budgeting, and strategic planning processes. Like other best-in-class or emerging experts in CPM, TransUnion is focusing significant resources on educating the organization to create awareness and understanding of the benefits of applying this discipline across all levels. The company has also adopted a technology tool that it hopes to use increasingly to help manage and optimize its individual investments and overall portfolio.

Of course, like many organizations, TransUnion aims to go after the elusive, but very rewarding area of benefits realization and performance measurement. "We want and need to look at benefits and expenses against and over the projected period. While time tracking is something we do from a resource perspective to view variances at a resource level, we need more tracking infrastructure in place to push our performance measurement competencies," contends Sanghani.

Finally, Sanghani and Madden continue to promote CPM within the organization from an engagement perspective at both a total company-level and senior-leadership level. While some notable areas and people heading up areas such as marketing, sales, and strategy are fully on board with CPM, there is still significant opportunity to galvanize additional support for it with the company's top brass. Sanghani wants to ensure that they have clearly defined the scope/boundaries of CPM, and within this defined range, his hope is that TransUnion will someday soon be practicing CPM enterprisewide.

HEWLETT-PACKARD[4]

Key Players

- Michael Menke, Chief Portfolio Advocate
- Kevin Yorks, Image and Printing Group (IPG) Portfolio Manager

Key Company Information

- Ticker: HPQ
- Market capitalization: $107B (as of 10/17/06)
- Revenue: $90+B annual revenue run rate (*Fortune* 11 company)
- Annual cash flow from operations: $8B[5]
- Annual operating expenses: $16.8B[6] (2005)
- Intellectual property: >30,000 patents
- Corporate structure: three major business segments
  - Personal systems group (PSG)—PCs, notebooks, handheld devices and workstations
  - Imaging and printing group (IPG)—printers, scanners, print servers, photo media
  - Technology solutions group (TSG)—servers, storage, infrastructure, consulting
- Positioning: Number 1 or 2 in virtually all markets it participates in

The top-level structure of Hewlett-Packard (HP) can be seen in Exhibit 4.3.

Company Profile

Hewlett-Packard Company provides products, technologies, solutions, and services to individual consumers, small and medium-sized businesses, and large enterprises worldwide. The company provides industry-standard servers and business-critical servers. It also offers entry-level, mid-range, and enterprise arrays; storage area networks; network attached storage; storage-management software; and virtualization technologies, as well as tape drives, tape libraries, and optical archival storage. In addition, HP provides multi-vendor information technology (IT) services, such as technology services, consulting and

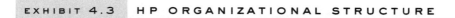

EXHIBIT 4.3   HP ORGANIZATIONAL STRUCTURE

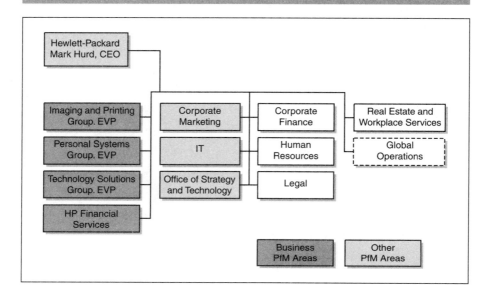

integration, managed services, and other services. In addition, the
company offers management software solutions that enable enterprise customers to manage their IT infrastructure, operations, applications, IT services, and business processes, as well as carrier-grade
platforms for developing and deploying voice, data, and converged
services to network and service providers. It offers commercial and
consumer personal computers, workstations, handheld computing
devices, digital entertainment systems, calculators and other related
accessories, as well as software and services; inkjet printers, LaserJet
printers, digital photography and entertainment, graphics, and imaging and printer supplies and accessories for printer hardware, digital
cameras, and scanning devices; and network infrastructure products,
including Ethernet switch products. Further, HP provides financial life
cycle management services. It also offers business process outsourc-
ing services, primarily in the area of payments, finances, accountability, and other IT services. The company sells its products through
retailers, distribution partners, independent distributors, original

equipment manufacturers, systems integrators, and systems integrators, as well as direct from the Web. HP was founded in 1939 by William R. Hewlett and David Packard. The company is headquartered in Palo Alto, California.[7]

HP and Portfolio Management: Brief History and Highlights

Of all the companies chronicled, HP has the longest history with portfolio management, having begun using it in the late 1990s. HP began using portfolio management on investment projects (PPM) and gradually has transitioned to using it on its businesses and their full range of investments (CPM). It started in the inkjet systems group to help the group make decisions about investments in major system technology platforms, which generally take three to four years and several hundred millions of dollars to develop. After their initial foray into project portfolio management (PPM), HP continued to use it in myriad capacities including the following areas:

- The Vancouver Division began using PPM to manage the development of new inkjet consumer printers (1999).
- Specialty Printing Systems applied a GE/McKinsey portfolio matrix to evaluate market opportunities (2000) in an early example of CPM.
- The server business defined a portfolio management decision architecture to bridge strategy and product development (2001).
- The laser jet unit began using a portfolio process to manage its product releases, and the digital imaging unit began to analyze its intellectual property portfolio (2002).
- HP corporate applied a portfolio process to compare the efficiency and effectiveness of research and development (R&D) spending all across HP at the request of the board of directors (2003 and 2006).
- In 2004 Enterprise Imaging and Printing and New Business Creation began using portfolio management.
- IPG Transformation and a corporate growth portfolio were defined in 2005 with CPM being an integral component of these efforts.

- Most recently, the graphics business used CPM to plan for growth projects, and IPG is specifically leveraging CPM to assess strategic shifts in its portfolio.

How and Why Did HP Embrace CPM So Significantly?

Given the previously mentioned utilizations of CPM within HP, what was it about HP which led to such widespread use of CPM? As Kevin Yorks and Michael Menke point out, "HP's use of CPM has been evolutionary, not revolutionary. Five to six years ago, we did an interesting study to benchmark the effectiveness of our R&D processes against that of other companies. What that showed us was that our actual R&D processes are quite good, but our processes to decide on what R&D initiatives to tackle were terrible." At a more tactical level, HP realized that there is a direct and critical linkage from an R&D perspective between the inkjet supplies and printer groups as these groups have intertwined fates. Surprisingly, however, there was no mechanism to tie the two together. The lack of a tie-up made it difficult for the supplies organization to determine what to invest in. This problem is made more acute because two to five years of investment in a supplies platform development initiative can have implications for 10 to 15 years, given the long product life cycles for these types of HP product platforms. In view of the need to sync up the supply and printer R&D processes, Yorks stated "This was one of the first realizations that portfolio management might be something the corporation needed."

As CPM evolved within HP, it then graduated to the Imaging & Printing Group's (IPG) senior management as they became very interested in looking at their business holistically. About three years ago (April 2004), the executive vice president of the group, Vyomesh Joshi, indicated that he would like to transform IPG to ensure continued success, and in order to do this, he needed to better understand where his best future opportunities were. In essence, Joshi wanted to adopt a portfolio management approach to evaluating and funding these opportunities. By leveraging a variety of inputs and statistics relevant to IPG, including market growth characteristics, financial expectations, market news, and so forth, the team developed a series of scorecards and criteria to understand these markets and, more importantly, understand HP's ability to compete in these markets. This effort to look at IPG through a portfolio lens was known within HP as IPG Transformation. As part of the Transformation initiative, portfolio management was used across the 27 existing and new strategic business units that comprise IPG, with each unit coming up with its strategic investment proposals along with the metrics (e.g., NPV, ROI, expenses, etc.) associated with those initiatives. Given the scale and required speed for this effort, the analysis was done at a more aggregate level. The unit subportfolios were then reviewed and optimized across IPG.

Regarding the results of this portfolio management effort within IPG, Yorks commented that "Transformation was looking at the totality of IPG. Some ideas were new and some got funded. Others got canned. And one or two things already in the portfolio got dropped or fundamentally changed." From his perspective, the exercise was important as the company is "continuously looking for new ideas and new businesses. We've been doing this for two years and have been fine-tuning the portfolio from low-growth to high-growth markets."

The work with IPG Transformation ultimately resulted in CPM's continued evolution within HP. Later in the same year, Menke was successful in getting another major unit to assimilate portfolio management into the fabric of its business. He proposed utilizing it for new opportunities, and in May 2006, the process was used to look at 30 to 50 conceptual opportunities that ultimately got weeded down to 30, of which 15 were studied at some level of granularity. This exercise also achieved a reasonable level of success and, as Menke put it, "The building blocks are now in place to put a total company process together."

Menke asserted, "With our work with IPG Transformation, we continued to notice the organic development of portfolio management within the organization. One of the units in IPG realized that they did not have an effective portfolio management discipline and so they set out to design one right before IPG Transformation initiative kicked off. Everyone realized, however, at this point that a portfolio management process was already built so the group that built the PM discipline pitched the project sponsor of this unit on the fact that we have already done this so you can just " 'adopt and go'." As we see it, portfolio management is a technique, philosophy, and strategy that can be applied at many different levels of the organization."

A more recent development has also emerged, with IPG noticing that it is not achieving its expectations of being number 1 in certain markets. To this end, 'IPG has called upon personnel to look at three to five large opportunity areas and develop a plan to achieve the company's goals in these areas. However, given finite resource availability, it has become important to build robust business cases for these opportunities as money, an always scarce resource, will need to be allocated to the most attractive opportunities.

In order to enable this, the company again has called for the utilization of a portfolio management approach leveraging some of its prior IPG experience as part of a two-step process. First, the company utilized a framework developed by GE/McKinsey to assess the conceptual opportunities before them (see Exhibit 4.4).

The framework served as an initial screen and conversation starter, which proved highly effective according to Menke and Yorks. Oftentimes, HP opportunity owners realized that their opportunities were not all that attractive after using this framework. Stated Menke, "There is a very rich set of opportunities that lie before HP, and it became fairly black and white as to what should or should not be investigated in detail."

One of the notable attributes that drove the success of this framework was the "open-book scoring" that was used, and the second step that required that participants justify their proposals to a core cross-functional team, which was composed of two people from business strategy, one financial lead, Yorks, and Menke. This team evaluated and reviewed the scoring and risk-return framework submitted by idea owners. There were five principal metrics utilized in evaluating investments including

1. Increasing shareholder value, as calculated using expected NPV
2. Return on investment (ROI), which is expected NPV divided by total discretionary incremental operating expenses and capital over several years
3. Short-term profit (also measured over several years)
4. Time to profitability
5. Risk

EXHIBIT 4.4   FRAMEWORK UTILIZED BY HP TO ASSESS

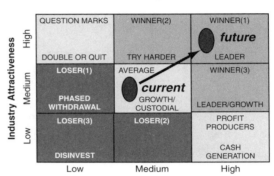

Market Attractiveness

- Market Size
- Market Growth
- Barriers to Entry
- Current Market Profit
- Future Profit Potential

 We can assess the strength of our business design alternatives for a given market. For example, we test our competitive strength score given our current capabilities then rescore based on our best future business design/strategic plan.

Business Strength and Competitiveness

- Current Market Share
- HP Brand
- Sustainable Technology Advantage
- Channels of Distribution Advantage
- Services Advantage
- Support Advantage
- Cost Structure Advantage

Challenges for Portfolio Management

Despite its significant progress as it relates to portfolio management, Menke and Yorks both intimated that they still have ambitious goals ahead with regard to making portfolio management part of the DNA of HP. As Menke pointed out "Portfolio management is currently thought of more as an exercise than a business practice." The team along with colleagues is hoping to change this and get wider acceptance of portfolio management across the organization.

IPG has also purchased a portfolio software application to replace the parade of spreadsheets previously being used. While the two contend that the tool has lived up to their expectations from a portfolio analysis perspective, it has not totally replaced the spreadsheets, which still take care of much of the heavy lifting to evaluate individual opportunities and businesses. As Yorks explained, "Most portfolio tools available today are for data aggregation and manipulation. They don't necessarily help you create the data, which is what spreadsheet models are still used for."

Menke and Yorks acknowledge that while portfolio management has been successful when used and taken seriously, it still has opportunities to break past these pockets of success. Yorks goes on to explain his hopes as follows, "We have made more informed decisions as a result of portfolio management, and we will continue to make better decisions because of it. It has helped us make decisions to go after some markets and this has helped galvanize the organization around the strategy. That said, there is an opportunity to use it more broadly across IPG and close the loop on decisions we've made. And while we use it a lot for R&D and business strategy, there is a marketing side of the equation we could also use it for."

Menke and Yorks remain undeterred by any obstacles to their progress as they see significant benefits accruing to the organization from adoption of these principles. They are attacking it in a bottoms-up way with a robust training curriculum that Menke has put together, which is made up of six modules presented over three intensive days. The training is focused on strategic financial analysis and references portfolio management as one of its central tenets. (*Note*: Details of this training are covered in more detail in the Appendix.)

As they create this bottoms-up support for CPM within HP, they both advise others moving down the CPM path to learn from their efforts by cautioning that "working these things bottoms-up is not always best. You need to bug senior management into seeing that they need to do better and that we have a process in CPM that can help you do better. Hopefully some of them will listen and become advocates going forward." To this end, Menke and Yorks have made progress developing at least one advocate in Joshi, who heads up IPG. Joshi now talks about his portfolio all the time. Declared Yorks, "He realizes this is one of his organizational challenges and that he needs a fair and credible way to discern what his best options are. Portfolio management enables this."

CISCO SYSTEMS

Key Players

- Dennis Powell, Chief Financial Officer and Senior Vice President
- Jonathan Chadwick, Controller, Vice President of Finance
- Betsy Rafael, Vice President, Corporate Finance
- Bill Bien, Senior Director, Strategic Planning/Corporate Finance

Key Company Information[8]

- Market capitalization: $165.4B
- Stock price: $27.25
- Forward P/E: 17.93
- PEG ratio (5-year expected): 1.28
- Revenue (ttm): $30.12B
- Net income (ttm): $5.93B
- Employees: 49,926

Company Profile[9]

Cisco Systems, Inc. designs, manufactures, and sells intellectual property (IP)—based networking and other products relating to the communications and information technology industry worldwide. It provides products for transporting data, voice, and video within buildings, across campuses, and around the world. It offers routers, which interconnect computer networks; and switching systems, which offer connectivity to end users, workstations, and servers. The company also offers application networking services products; home networking products, such as voice and data modems, network cards, media adapters, Internet video cameras, and USB adapters; and hosted small-business systems, including integrated voice and data products. In addition, it provides optical networking products; network security products and services; storage area networking products; Unified Communications, an integrated system that provides voice, video, data, and Web services; and video systems that consist of digital set-top boxes, digital media technology products, and transport and access products. Further, the company offers in-building and outdoor wireless networking products, such as access points, wireless LAN controllers, wireless management software, wireless LAN clients and client software, bridges, antennas, and accessories; and service provider IP communications and network management software products. The company offers its products and services through its direct sales force, systems integrators, service providers, other resellers, distributors, and retail partners. It has strategic alliances with Accenture, Ltd.; AT&T Corp.; BearingPoint, Inc.; Cap Gemini S.A.; Electronic Data Systems Corporation; EMC Corporation; Ericsson; Fujitsu Limited; Hewlett-Packard Company; Intel Corporation; International Business Machines Corporation; Italtel SpA; Microsoft Corporation; Motorola, Inc.; Siemens AG; and Sprint Nextel Corporation. The company was founded in 1984 and is headquartered in San Jose, California.

A Need to Create an Enterprise View

"Cisco's philosophy under John Chambers has been to empower and trust its leaders, and as a result, our goals are visionary and strategic," according to Bill Bien, senior director of strategic planning and corporate finance at Cisco. As Cisco has grown in size and complexity, however, its executive team identified a need to align cross-functional strategies and execution plans to ensure a common vision. To accomplish this objective, senior leadership wanted to create a simple and comprehensive long-range planning process that would continue the sense of ownership and empowerment over various subportfolios within the company but would also provide broader visibility into total company strategy and performance. The leadership wanted a process that would enable review of an ongoing three-year strategic plan and increase accountability and dialog across the company.

As an organization, Cisco moved to the following functional hierarchy four years ago (Exhibit 4.5):

- Sales
- Engineering
- Marketing
- Service
- Operations, processes, and systems
- Finance

EXHIBIT 4.5   CISCO BUSINESS MODEL:
FUNCTIONAL VIEW

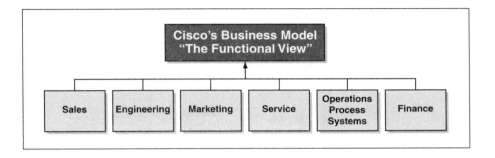

As Bien stated, "We started to find that we were optimized for efficiencies within functions, but we also saw an opportunity to execute decisions across customer segments." In line with this desire, the company also established three councils for the company's major customer segments which included:

- **Service provider council.** Focus is on telecom companies.
- **Enterprise council.** Focus is on *Fortune* 5000 companies.
- **Commercial council.** Focus is on mid-market and small-market companies (at least 100 employees)

There is also a consumer business composed of Cisco businesses (e.g., Linksys, Scientific Atlanta), but there is not a council for this area. Cisco's organizational setup from a customer perspective is shown in Exhibit 4.6.

"The Councils help us respond to market, product, and customer needs. They proactively launch new solutions, respond rapidly to market changes, agree on investment goals, manage performance, and align our Go-to-Market (GTM) and engineering efforts for important initiatives," according to Bien.

The functional and council views of the business allow the company to consider different perspectives for long-range planning, specifically:

- Different growth expectations
- Different investments and return profiles

EXHIBIT 4.6 CISCO BUSINESS MODEL: CUSTOMER SEGMENT VIEW

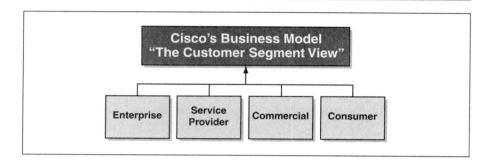

- Different go-to-market needs
- Varying product expectations and strategies
- Core processes tailored to customer experience

As a part of strategic planning, the issue Cisco faced was that functional and customer views were not formally tied to a corporate budget; while you could get a yes for an initiative; it was not always tied to resource allocations at year end. For effective alignment, there needed to be a balance between functions and councils. Cisco's solution was to establish an executive operating committee in 2004, composed of Cisco's top executives, to proactively balance issues and opportunities across the entire enterprise.

Goals of the Operating Committee Model

Operating Committee and Long-Range Planning Two tools were created to support the operating committee: a cross-functional long-range planning process and the operating committee dashboard. To understand the ultimate goals of the operating committee, it is essential to understand the intentions of Cisco's long-range planning process, which is predicated on the main goal of increasing long-term profitable growth. To this end, the company has stated the need to have

- A better customer-segmented view of business performance and goals

- An understanding and agreement on the company's business model (P&L, process/systems) by segment
- A means to fund and resource priorities
- A way to provide for unpredicted risks and opportunities

At a tactical level, the operating committee is a formal review between Cisco's most senior personnel on a monthly basis to talk about resource allocation and strategic issues. The organizational view of the company following the implementation of the operating committee is provided in Exhibit 4.7.

EXHIBIT 4.7 CISCO'S ORGANIZATIONAL STRUCTURE

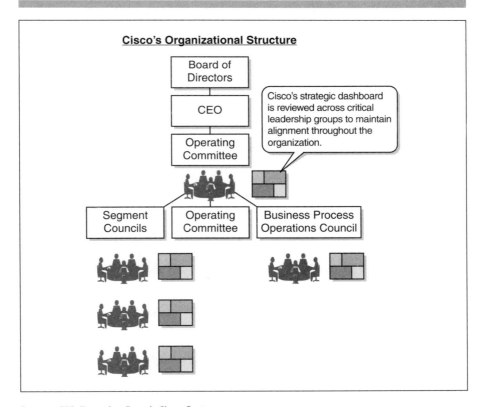

Source: CFO Executive Board, Cisco Systems

Bien added that "the central task at monthly Operating Committee meetings is essential reviews of Cisco's business and long-term strategy."

- **Business review.** This review focuses on current product forecasts and the impact of sales, engineering, and manufacturing trends on the forecast. Decisions are then made at each meeting to optimize the company's chances to meet or beat mid-term bookings forecasts.

- **Corporate strategy review.** This review focuses on aligning resources to the appropriate long-term initiatives to achieve shareholder goals. It also looks at macro-changes such as changes in customer behavior, new technology introductions, and new growth avenues for the company. Both the customer segment councils and the operating committee apply this approach to their respective topics. These two reviews give Cisco a holistic sense of the business and ensure alignment around all its essential strategic areas including

  - Corporate strategy
  - Customer segment strategies
  - Functional strategies
  - Operational strategies
  - Communication strategies

Given the seniority of members of the operating committee, the portfolio discussions around resource allocation focus on initiatives that are material to a company the size of Cisco (i.e., several hundred million dollars). "We empower the councils and functional groups to make decisions on most investments to encourage entrepreneurial leadership" clarified Bien. Resource allocation and management are key elements of each operating committee segment council meeting as these decisions ultimately drive Cisco's growth and profitability. Resource constraints are considered to develop a unified recommendation that links long-term strategy to short-term investments so that key initiatives, the overall business, and important operational investments are all supported. Exhibit 4.8 shows the view Cisco uses when considering resource allocation questions.

EXHIBIT 4.8   CISCO'S RESOURCE ALLOCATION
CONSIDERS ORGANIZATIONAL
CONSTRAINTS

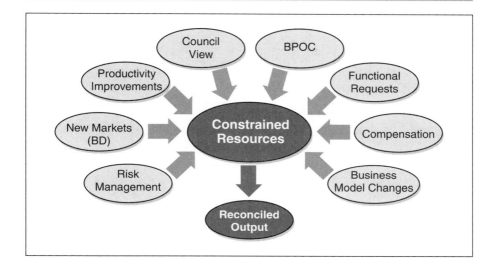

Operating Committee Dashboard   Monthly operating committee dashboard meetings serve as the precursor to a quarterly review of the
strategic dashboard with a subset of the operating committee. In
putting the initial dashboard together, Cisco aimed to keep it simple.
"Balanced Scorecard theory says you have to measure lots of different
things. Many balanced scorecards fall under their own weight, unable
to represent a straightforward, meaningful indicator of achievement,"
stated Bien. Keeping this pitfall in mind, the team at Cisco targeted
metrics that were most significant, using several general principles:

"With the initiation of the operating committee dashboard, we
tried to keep it practical and uncomplicated. We didn't seek to tie it
to long range planning in the beginning. Instead, its purpose was to
help the Operating Committee identify key business issues and track
performance. We designed it with John's [Chambers] top five executive leaders to gain their buy-in. The result was a dashboard that
differs from a typical balanced scorecard. It measures lagging metrics
that assess and emphasize growth, profitability, market share, product

quality, and customer satisfaction across product, customer and geographical views of the business. We didn't initially assign goals to each metric. Instead, we used each dashboard view as a group troubleshooting and discussion tool. This approach was important at first to gain acceptance across the committee to measure new performance indicators. After five quarters of review, the executive team now accepts the new metrics and finds them useful," asserts Bien. The Cisco operating committee dashboard design criteria and reporting views are shown in Exhibits 4.9 and 4.10.

Benefits Realization and Strategy Reformulation

While the focus is on strategy at the monthly and quarterly operating committee meetings, there is significant effort and emphasis placed on understanding benefits realization and how the company is doing against stated goals and objectives.

EXHIBIT 4.9   CISCO'S DASHBOARD DESIGN CRITERIA

┌─────────────────── **METRIC SELECTION CRITERIA** ───────────────────┐

Universal Applicability
- Must have cross-enterprise relevance
- Must inform operating and strategy discussions

- -

Ease of Use
- Must fit on three sheets of paper; no complicated IT platform
- Easily quantifiable metrics
- Simple (not superficial) measures of value

- -

Clear Measures of Performance
- Unambiguous raw numbers; no hiding behind averages
- Lagging indicators that can be tracked frequently

EXHIBIT 4.10   CISCO'S REPORTING VIEWS
PROVIDE VISIBILITY INTO RESULTS

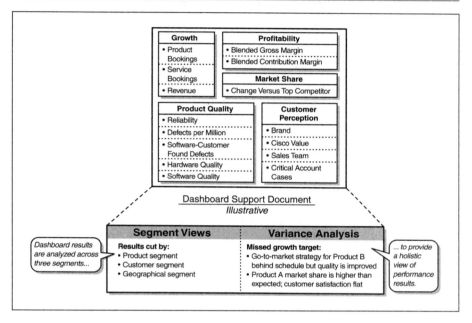

Source: CFO Executive Board, Cisco Systems

Every six months, an overall initiative assessment is provided that details progress, risks, and so on. Leaders who are responsible for priorities and goals also provide monthly updates. The dashboard that Bien's group put together serves to track all identified metrics by product, customer, and geography.

At bi-annual sessions, the councils also revisit corporate strategy. "Autonomy is important so strategy owners have significant discretion in modifying their plan based on needs. Formally, however, new strategies are proposed one time a year," added Bien.

Progress and Next Steps

The goal of the operating committee structure was to provide greater visibility at a corporate level, and, according to Bien, "it has definitely helped in raising the level, frequency, and value of company-wide conversations." Cisco is able to optimize its portfolio and align resource allocation with the company's stated strategic objectives.

The outcome of the new long-range planning process is a specific list of high-level priorities for the company that considers functional and customer objectives (see Exhibit 4.11).

From this list of priorities, the committee identifies investment opportunities based on overall importance and ease of implementation, as shown in Exhibit 4.12.

Going forward, the aim of Bien and his team is to keep pushing the envelope to formalize the long-range planning process over time. "We did it incrementally last year [2005] and to some degree, it was being designed as we went. It was a big change management effort. Now that we have the design down, we'll be looking to provide more forward looking guidance 6 to 12 months ahead of time."

Additionally, Bien says they are working on, "putting more upfront constraints into the process so it is less blue sky and more rigorous. The hope is that more finance time will be spent on the one year execution plan."

EXHIBIT 4.11   CISCO USES A FUNCTIONAL AND CUSTOMER VIEW TO DEVELOP PRIORITIES

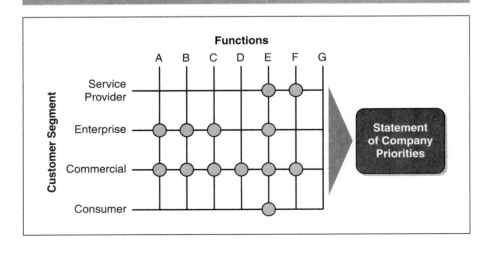

EXHIBIT 4.12 CISCO INVESTMENT EVALUATION FRAMEWORK

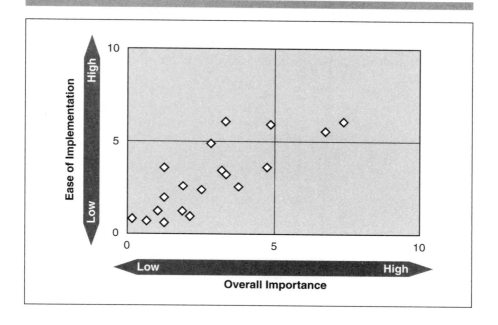

Cisco and CPM

Cisco Systems has adopted a corporate portfolio management discipline that is higher-level in its scope than many other companies. It does not focus on viewing a portfolio as composed of smaller initiatives, but instead looks at its portfolio from a strategic perspective. This is very much in line with the culture of autonomy and empowerment that John Chambers has brought to the company.

The monthly operating committee and quarterly dashboard meetings that Cisco holds ensure that issues and opportunities within the subportfolios are addressed in a timely and appropriate manner by allowing constant revisiting of resource allocation and strategic imperatives. The company's explicit tying of resource allocation to strategy along with the operating committee's conformity with and the company's cross-functional and collaborative leadership style is one of the hallmarks of a robust corporate portfolio management discipline.

The strategic and operational perspective that the operating committee provides to evaluate emerging threats and opportunities seems to be working, given recent company performance. Since the beginning of 2006, Cisco's stock price has gone up nearly 56%.[10] Year over year, quarterly revenue and earnings growth have been 24.9% and 27.5%, respectively.[11]

STATE OF OREGON DEPARTMENT OF HUMAN SERVICES

Key Participants

OREGON DEPARTMENT OF HUMAN SERVICES

- Fariborz Pakseresht—Chief Administrative Officer
- Bill Crowell—Chief Information Officer
- Dennis Wells—Manager, Policy and Planning
- Darren Wellington—Business Case Development
- Janet Gerling—Policy and Governance Formulation
- Nancy McIntyre—Strategic Planning and Performance Management

OREGON DEPARTMENT OF ADMINISTRATIVE SERVICES

- Sean McSpaden—Strategic IT Investment Manager, EISPD

The State of Oregon Department of Human Services (ODHS) approaches many aspects of its mission in a pioneering way. Its approach and utilization of corporate portfolio management (CPM) is also helping to break new ground in the use of this discipline within the public sector. To understand CPM's applicability at ODHS, it is useful to first understand the organization and its mission, values, objectives, and organizational structure.

Key Organizational Information

The Oregon legislature created the Oregon Department of Human Services in 1971 by bringing together the state's principal human services agencies. The department, with more than 9,400 positions and a 2005–07 budget of more than $9.9 billion administers more than 250 programs. Program funding sources are generated through the state's General Fund, Lottery Funds, Other Funds, and Federal Funds and approved through the Legislatively Approved Budget. ODHS is headquartered in Salem, OR.

The ODHS mission is "Helping people to become independent, healthy and safe."

This mission statement sets out the purpose and guides the activities of this large, complex organization. In support of the mission and to gauge its progress and organize and prioritize its work efforts, ODHS has established four broad goals. Each is supported in turn by specific, measurable outcomes that the department strives to achieve. This approach—stating goals, measuring results, and reporting progress to the public—reflects the department's commitment to better outcomes for clients and communities and behaviorally it is consistent with organizations that succeed in deploying CPM. Because many clients have multiple needs, the department is integrating services, seeking to bring a broad range of supports within easy reach of each client or family. This approach, recognized as pioneering in the nation, requires close collaboration among staff within the department and with local governments, service providers, and other partners.

The mission statement, the goals, and the values reflect ODHS' commitment to that vision.

ODHS Mission, Goals, and Core Values

- **Vision:** Better outcomes for clients and communities through collaboration, integration, and shared responsibility
- **Mission:** Assisting people to become independent, healthy, and safe
- **Goals:**
- People are healthy.
  - People are living as independently as possible.
  - People are safe.
  - People are able to support themselves and their families.
- **Core Values:** ODHS is a values-driven organization. At ODHS five core values are at the heart of who they are, what they do, and how they perform. ODHS aspires to have a workforce that aligns their actions with these core values.
  - Integrity
  - Stewardship
  - Responsibility
  - Respect
  - Professionalism

ODHS Structure

ODHS is made up of five divisions

1. **Children, Adults, and Families Division (CAF).** This division is responsible for administering self-sufficiency and child-protective programs. These include JOBS, Temporary Assistance for Needy Families (TANF), Employment Related Day Care, Food Stamps, child-abuse investigation and intervention, foster care, and adoptions. The group also contains the Office of Vocational Rehabilitation Services (OVRS), which helps Oregonians with disabilities to prepare for, find, and retain jobs. CAF Field Services is responsible for providing benefits and services to clients for the majority of ODHS programs. Field Services operates more than 110 offices across the state and employs more than half of the department's staff.

2. **Addictions and Mental Health Division (AMH).** This division is responsible for delivering adult and children's mental health and addiction services. Mental health services are delivered locally through community mental health departments and organizations, as well as through state-operated psychiatric hospitals. The division is responsible for delivering addiction prevention and treatment services in the areas of alcohol, tobacco, other drugs, and problem gambling.

3. **Public Health Division (PHD).** This division administers low-income medical programs. It provides public health services such as monitoring drinking water quality and communicable disease outbreaks and inspecting restaurants. The PHD also maintains the state's vital records, immunization services, and the WIC nutrition program—delivered through county health departments.

4. **Division of Medical Assistance Programs (DMAP).** This division oversees the Oregon Health Plan, which is a public/private partnership that ensures universal access to a basic level of health care for Oregonians. The division also includes provisions for oversight, research, and analysis to achieve the best use of health care funding.

5. **Seniors and People with Disabilities Division (SPD).** This division is responsible for the administration of programs that increase the independence of, and help protect, seniors and people with disabilities. Its functions include abuse investigation, licensing of nursing facilities, help in arranging and paying for in-home services, Oregon Project Independence, and Lifespan Respite. SPD also handles in-home, group-home, and crisis services for people with developmental disabilities. Another SPD function is eligibility determination for federal Social Security Disability benefits.

These five divisions are supported by three support divisions, which include

1. **The Director's Office**, which provides overall guidance, communication, and direction for ODHS. The director and deputy director are ultimately accountable for the Department's success.

2. **Finance and Policy Analysis (FPA),** which provides budget and forecasting services, monitors federal and state policies for their impact on the department's budget, and develops the rates paid to providers in DHS programs.

3. **Administrative Services Division (ASD)**, which serves the entire department with functions that include contracting, facilities, financial services, forms and document management, human resources, and information systems.

Within ASD is the Office of Information Services (OIS), lead by the department Chief Information Officer (CIO). OIS is composed of a small Administrative Support group and four operating entities: (1) Applications Maintenance and Support, (2) Customer Service and Support, (3) Strategic Systems Initiatives, and (4) IT Consulting Services. The OIS mission is to provide exceptional information services committed to fulfilling the DHS mission.

Through the management and use of state-of-the-art information systems technology and the establishment of statewide standards-based systems operations, OIS strengthens the DHS mission by providing information services to DHS operational divisions and the departmentwide support divisions.

With a total biennial budget of $169 million and more than 390 employees, OIS provides statewide services to more than 350 locations, including more than 140 DHS offices statewide, the Division of Child Support (a division of the Department of Justice), the Employment Department, cities, counties, other computer centers, other state agencies, other states, private hospitals, district attorney offices, and other entities. OIS services the more than 9,500 users, maintains and supports more than 8,500 computer devices, provides technical support for the security of data and reliability of more than 15,500 databases and files, and manages more than 500 network connections.

Evolution of CPM within Oregon

Governance Mechanisms   The state of Oregon has been involved in the development of corporate portfolio management since before 2001. A number of state agencies, including ODHS lead by the Department of Administrative Services (DAS), coordinated efforts, which ultimately grew and evolved into IT Portfolio Management. A law requiring IT Portfolio Management (HB3372) was signed in August 2001. Substantive provisions of the law were included in ORS 184.470–184.477. HB3372 and ORS 184.470 state, "IT Portfolio Management (i.e., IT investment management) is an integral approach to managing investments that provides for the continuous identification, selection, control life-cycle management, and evaluation of investments."

DAS Enterprise Information Strategy and Policy Division (EISPD) supports the State CIO and IT-related governance bodies. The division leads state government in enterprise information technology management, strategic planning, and policy. IT Investment and Planning (ITIP) leads statewide IT planning and budgeting; develops and implements state IT management strategies, rules, policies, standards, and processes. ITIP is responsible for the state's IT portfolio and asset-management program. EISPD (created in September 2006, formerly Information Resources Management Division) initially developed a two-phase initiative to comply with the ORS.

IT Asset Management   The first phase of this important state government-wide initiative involved the

- Definition and development of the rules, policies, standards, and guidelines required for the tracking and reporting of assets owned by state agencies.

- Creation of an Enterprise IT Asset Management Program within DAS/EISPD.
- Identification and documentation of the requirements for an IT Asset Management System within DAS/EISPD (e.g., repository, auto-discovery tools, software usage tools, etc.).
- Creation of statewide pricing agreements for IT Asset Management tools and services.
- Collection of an initial inventory of state agency IT assets.

While phase 1 was planned to be completed in the 2003–05 biennium, some elements of the phase carried over into the 2005–07 biennium.

One of the significant deliverables from phase 1 was the IT Asset Inventory/Management Policy, DAS IRM 107-004-010. State law requires the DAS EISPD to ensure that all state-owned information technology (IT) assets are inventoried, tracked, and managed throughout the IT asset's life cycle. This policy provides the governance mechanism to ensure compliance with state law and provide oversight for and management of the IT Asset Management program.

IT Portfolio (Investment) Management   The second phase of the initiative (to be completed in the 2005–07 biennium) will allow DAS and state agencies to fulfill the legislative intent of ORS 184.473 through 184.477 (IT Portfolio Management; IT Asset Inventory and Management) by

- Developing state government–wide standards, processes, and procedures for the management of the state government–wide IT portfolio and conducting and maintaining a continuous inventory of each state agency's IT (a compilation of information about those assets and the total life cycle cost of those assets).
- Conducting and subsequently maintaining that state government–wide inventory.
- Creating an Enterprise IT Portfolio (Investment) Management Program within DAS/EISPD.
- Integrating state agency strategic and business planning, technology planning and budgeting, and project expenditure

> processes into the Enterprise IT Portfolio (Investment) Management Program.

- Ensuring that state agencies implement portfolio-based management of information technology resources in accordance with ORS 184.473 through 184.477 and with rules adopted by the DAS Director.

State IT Strategy   The state continues to drive the corporate portfolio management initiative through the state Enterprise Information Resources Management Strategy (EIRMS). The EIRMS is a business-driven IT planning process designed to address common business needs, specifically: supporting achievement of the Governor's Oregon Principles, supporting strategic business objectives of state agencies, and providing a common vision of the planning, staffing, acquisition, management, and shared use of IT throughout Oregon government. There are three goals and objectives identified within the strategy that are integral to implementing, enabling, achieving, and sustaining enterprise portfolio management throughout the state, as outlined in the following text:

Goal 1: Establish effective business-driven Enterprise IT Governance

Objective 1.1: Implement the state's IT Governance Policy

Goal 2: Optimize the efficiency and effectiveness of government

Objective 2.1: Establish a facts-based continuous improvement and performance management program

Goal 3: Ensure IT investments are selected, resourced, acquired, and tracked to optimize mission accomplishment

Objective 3.1: Implement an IT investment (portfolio) management program as required by ORS 184.470–184.477

Department of Human Services Perspective

Despite the well-informed intentions of lawmakers, HB3372 was an unfunded mandate. Implementing portfolio management is not a trivial undertaking. Within ODHS it is even more challenging. There were no resources aligned with the bill. In October 2004 the OIS Policy and Planning team within ODHS, as an agent of DAS, was drafting a Request for Proposal (RFP) for a portfolio-management software application. Unfortunately there were no foundational processes in place to govern the practice and discipline of portfolio management. So the obvious question that was asked was, "what are we enabling?" Without a clear understanding of what portfolio management is, best practices, and how the IT department and the agency can leverage the decision support attributes that portfolio management provides, there was little utility in investing in an application. As a result, ODHS changed direction and has been focusing on developing and implementing the governance and component processes to drive portfolio management.

The OIS Policy and Planning team initiated their efforts by developing a business case template, now in its second iteration. Near-simultaneous to this effort was a collaborative policy development initiative with the Financial and Policy Analysis business unit. The result was ODHS Policy DHS-110-001, Information Technology Project Budgets. The policy explicitly requires the development of a formal business case for any business investment opportunity that may have an IT component and that will require budget/limitation authority transfer to the Office of Information Services. It is also intended that all DHS-approved Policy Option Packages (POPs) will require a completed business. POPs are developed and used by state agencies to identify new investment opportunities and are a vehicle to develop their agency budgets.

The business-case development effort admittedly got off to a rough start and initially created some bad feelings and discontent. Since its initial public offering, a governance process, process flow, business-case guidelines, and a business-case development facilitation process have been developed and implemented. Business-case development has evolved into a collaborative effort within ODHS showing the following characteristics:

- It is business driven, led by the business or program area that is initiating the proposal.
- Information technology representative(s) form the Office of Information Services.
- It has financial analyst representative(s) from Finance Policy and Analysis.

- It embraces any (all) stakeholders who will be impacted by the proposal to ensure approval and ongoing support
- It has a benefits sponsor.

Within the business case, ODHS identifies typical financial metrics including return on income (ROI), net present value (NPV), internal rate of return (IRR), with ROI being the most utilized. Given that ODHS's vision and mission are more altruistic in nature, ODHS also heavily discusses and aims to capture metrics on public value (i.e., what benefit does this investment have for the public).

Although there is still some angst around building a business case for investment opportunities, agency leadership has developed an appreciation for the due diligence, rigor, consistency, and information that business cases contribute to the decision-making process.

ODHS also has in place an IT Governance Council (ITGC). ITGC is growing increasingly comfortable and confident in its role as an investment review board. The membership includes all assistant deputy directors of the operational and departmentwide support divisions along with the CIO, deputy CIO, and key support staff from Policy and Planning. Without using specific portfolio-management terminology, the ITGC is asking for all the components and best practices of portfolio management; how they see or gain visibility into all projects or investments, how they select or differentiate an investment initiative from one division against an investment opportunity from another division, what is the resources allocation, what is the organizational capacity, and so forth. Most encouraging is that the questions are not IT specific. ODHS's business partners are equally concerned with business capacity and business resources. The ITGC is maturing to taking a holistic view of its role beyond specific divisional goals and objectives.

Results, Challenges, and Next Steps
Since implementing the business-case process, ODHS has evaluated 33 business cases influencing governance decision for projects totaling $94 million. Beyond this review process, there are several benefits of having an evolving CPM discipline within the organization including

- A cultural shift around the value of doing business cases; there is increasing recognition that while developing a business case may be challenging and time consuming, there is inherent value in knowing the value proposition, risks, benefits, costs, and so on of any investment.

- Driving the agency leadership to do the right thing.
- Alignment with the ODHS core values; integrity, responsibility and accountability, and stewardship.

The efforts of ODHS are not without the challenges that any CPM effort brings, including

- Education and awareness of CPM and its benefits, which remains the top challenge faced by ODHS. The lack of understanding leads to further confusion regarding the benefits of what the discipline will do for people individually and ODHS overall
- Defining portfolios; there are varying perceptions of what a portfolio is, but there is no concerted effort to define and manage portfolios.
- Evolving a link between strategic planning, performance management, and portfolio management.

In terms of where ODHS envisions CPM going forward, ODHS hopes to achieve several goals and objectives, as outlined in the following list.

- Most immediately, the CPM work will feed into the budget development process, which is being done for 2007–09 budget cycle. ODHS's CPM effort has a direct tie to the agency's proposed budget, which serves as a major input into the governor's recommended budget. The goal is that new resources will be allocated to ODHS as part of the Legislatively Approved Budget.
- Additional components of portfolio management need to be developed and implemented—selection criteria, prioritization (weighting and scoring mechanism), the portfolio review process (and in the case of the project portfolio, a link to the project management process), resource and capacity planning, and benefits realization.

- The strategic planning process should be aligned with the budget cycle to enable the portfolio management process to better and more directly influence programming, planning, budgeting, and execution.
- A final goal is to expand the portfolio management practices and discipline beyond IT investments to include all agency spending.

Conclusion

Oregon and specifically DHS continue to push on their CPM efforts and their attempts to make data-centric, business-case–driven decisions about investments. This is worthy of praise on many levels but especially because they continue to bring a businesslike approach to CPM, keeping in mind their ultimate objective to serve as stewards for public trust while trying to achieve the mission of keeping people safe, healthy. and independent.

If you consider that many large, for-profit entities have not even begun to scratch the surface when it comes to CPM, the progressive and forward-thinking people within Oregon's government—and specifically within DHS—are impressive. Similarly, ODHS takes consolation in its slow but steady progress. They point to a recognized expert in portfolio management who emphasizes working on process development, implementation, and practice from one to two years before investing in a commercial software solution. The objective is for the solution to be configured to an organization's processes and best practices.

Oregon will also readily admit that it is not the most or the only progressive state aiming to implement portfolio management practices. North Carolina, Virginia, Utah, Nevada, and Wisconsin are just a few of the states Oregon has spoken to concerning portfolio management practices. Nor is ODHS the only agency within Oregon to pursue this effort. There are several others at various levels of maturity, setting the example, balancing their investments, and doing the right thing.

Notes

1. Yahoo Finance, ticker: AXP (as of 11/10/06).
2. Yahoo Finance, ticker: AXP.
3. All the information in this case study, unless cited otherwise, comes from TransUnion company presentations or from an interview with TransUnion personnel.
4. All the information in this case study, unless cited otherwise, comes from HP company presentations or interviews with HP personnel.
5. HP company presentation, APQC Benchmarking, September 27, 2006.
6. Yahoo Finance, http://finance.yahoo.com/q/pr?s=HPQ.
7. Yahoo Finance, http://finance.yahoo.com/q/pr?s=HPQ.
8. Yahoo Finance, ticker: CSCO (as of 12/13/06)
8. Yahoo Finance, ticker: CSCO (as of 12/13/06)
10. SmartMoney Select as of 11/10/06
11. Yahoo Finance, ticker: CSCO, considers trailing twelve months ending July 29, 2006

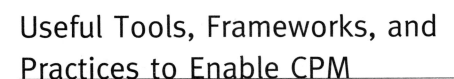

Useful Tools, Frameworks, and Practices to Enable CPM

PERSONNEL SURVEY: UNDERSTANDING CURRENT COMPANY PRACTICES AND ATTITUDES TOWARD CPM

Note: The attached memo and questionnaire should be customized to your needs and objectives. This survey is intended for organizations who have decided to utilize a corporate portfolio management (CPM) discipline. Given this decision, the aim of this survey is to gauge your organization's process and behavioral readiness for CPM by polling several key individuals and stakeholders about current company practices and their understanding and attitudes regarding CPM. It can also be used within organizations that have already undertaken CPM and want to see how they are doing. You will notice that it is constructed for an organization looking to do total company portfolio management, and it is fairly high level. If you want to apply this to a subgroup or single business unit within your organization, you can use it for those purposes with some customization. A memo may be unnecessary in many organizations, and the survey is best utilized as the guide for a discussion with the right people in the room. Sending out the survey is advisable if geographic distance or the scope of the effort are too large to allow for in-person discussion. If conducting an in-person meeting, you should utilize some of the meeting guidelines previously discussed.

MEMO

Dear Colleague,

As you may know, we have recently undertaken an effort to improve our decision-making abilities by utilizing a corporate portfolio management (CPM) discipline. At a high level, CPM is an effort to look at an organization as a portfolio of projects and initiatives with the aim of selecting the best projects or initiatives while considering near- and long-term strategic, financial, and risk objectives. To further this effort, we've developed the following brief survey, which we are sending around the organization to help us understand how we currently allocate resources and to gather your feedback on how this process works and what can be retained or improved over time. Specifically, the survey hopes to find out

- Your familiarity with CPM
- Your organization's familiarity with CPM
- How resources are currently allocated within your organization
- What your organization's strengths are with respect to its decision-making processes
- What the development areas of your organization are with reference to managing its portfolio of investments

The survey should not take you more than 20 minutes to complete.

It is not expected that you would know the answers to all these questions conclusively, but even your informed, educated opinions are extremely valuable. I want to stress that your honest assessment of your organization will ensure that our efforts are most efficient and targeted.

Thanks very much for taking the time to fill out this survey. If you have any questions, comments, or ideas, don't hesitate to contact me at (insert contact info)

Warm regards,

Your name
Title
Company

Instructions: Fields marked in gray should be filled in.

Organization Details and Background

Your Information

Name	
Title	
Group	
Telephone	
Email	
Fax	
Other	
Alternative email	

Gauging Organizational Readiness: Behavior

Terminology: The term corporate portfolio management (CPM) often is referred to using different terms within different organizations. Some alternatives include resource allocation, investment optimization, capital planning, among others. Within your organization, what terms are used to describe resource allocation, if any?

Organizational engagement: CPM can impact all parts of an organization. To this end, can you tell us how different parts of your organization view CPM and its importance? Place an 'X' in the appropriate box. (1—not at all important to 7—extremely important or NA—if CPM is not used or understood in this area.)

Increasing importance ──────────→

	1	2	3	4	5	6	7	NA
Total company engagement								
Finance								
• Corporate Finance/Planning								
• Budgeting, Planning, and Forecasting								
• Enterprise Risk								
Strategic Planning								
Information Technology								
R&D/Innovation								
Marketing and Advertising								
Sales								
Operations								
Reengineering								
M&A/Corporate Development								
Other #1*:								
Other #2*:								
Other #3*:								

Senior leadership engagement: How important an issue to your organization's senior leadership is CPM? Provide your estimate of the importance various senior leaders place on resource allocation. Place an 'X' in the appropriate box. (1—Not a priority, 7—A top priority)

Increasing importance ⟶

	1	2	3	4	5	6	7	NA
CEO								
CFO								
CIO								
CTO								
CMO/Head of marketing								
Head of research								
Head of operations								
Head of strategy								
Other #1★:								
Other #2★:								
Other #3★:								

★As organizations are often set up quite differently, these fields are for you to mention other groups and/or senior leaders that are not captured within the survey already.

For the next set of questions, please put an 'X' next to the answer that best describes your organization.

Within our industry, our organization probably is

—best-in-class when it comes to CPM

—better than most when it comes to CPM

—average in regard to CPM

—below average in regard to CPM

Relative to other organizations across all industries, we probably are

—best-in-class when it comes to CPM.

—better than most when it comes to CPM

—average in regard to CPM

—below average in regard to CPM

Within our organization,

—we have a process in place to view our
corporate portfolio at a total company level.

—portions of the organization have established
processes to evaluate their investment portfolios.

—we do not have a process to evaluate corporate
portfolios at either a total or a partial company level.

If parts of your organization have a CPM process, indicate which specific areas have this discipline (business segments, functional groups, product areas, etc.):

With regard to a technology solution to aid in our CPM discipline, we

—have a solution in place to help with CPM.

—are evaluating a technology solution to aid in managing our CPM.

—think a solution may be required but have not done any work on this front at present.

—are not at a point where a technology solution is needed.

—do not think technology is required to help in the management of the CPM discipline.

If using a technology or evaluating one for helping with your CPM processes, indicate which one(s) in the following space.

When it comes to CPM, our organization

—has a good understanding of the importance of this discipline.

—has parts that understand the importance of CPM.

—does not recognize or has not understood the importance of CPM.

To ensure that people are aligned and doing what is best for the organization and not just their area or business segment,

—we have the appropriate incentives in place
(i.e., no silos.)

—we are working on implementing processes and
practices that will ensure this.

—nothing is being done currently to align incentives
with optimal CPM.

—we do not see a link between CPM optimization
and incentives.

If a CPM discipline could help you achieve three objectives, what would they be?

1

2

3

When you think of someone implementing a CPM discipline within the organization, what challenges do you think they will face?

When you discuss CPM within your organization, what resources are you mainly speaking about and hoping to optimize resource allocation of? (Please put an 'x' next to any item that applies to your organization.)

Money

Time

People

Operational capacity

Other(s)

Do you feel CPM is a concept understood within your organization?

Yes   No

If yes, what do you think has driven this understanding?
If no, what are the challenges and impediments involved in this understanding?

In regard to CPM, what practices, processes, and so forth does your organization already have that may lend themselves to adopting a CPM discipline?

Thank you for taking the time to fill out this survey.

HP's Strategic Financial Analysis Curriculum Outline

In the changing organizational behavior section of Chapter 2, educating decision makers across the organization was essential for changing their behavior. What follows is a summarized version of Hewlett-Packard's (HP's) training program, which talks about resource allocation and portfolio management. However, it goes well beyond those topics in the effort to educate its workforce. This program is amongst the most comprehensive training curricula I've seen.

Strategic Financial Analysis Training Program

The goal of this program is to improve the skills and capabilities of HP executives, marketing, finance, and strategy people in decision making, strategy development, alternative generation, business models, business design, decision quality, decision and risk analysis, and portfolio management. The course covers the complete set of processes and methods to identify good choices for allocating scarce resources to maximize shareholder value in a dynamic, uncertain environment. The approach aligns directly with the HP Standards of Performance Excellence. While initially developed for the Imaging and Printing Group (IPG), this program is relevant to all members of the management, finance, and planning community across HP who are involved in making and/or preparing important decisions. The benefit will be developing, evaluating, and selecting the best strategic alternatives to recommend to HP management for HP's future success.

The modules (each designed for four hours) are as follows:

1. Introduction to Strategy and Decision Quality: Executive Overview—this module defines the core concepts of decision, strategy, and decision quality and provides an overview of the philosophy, process, methodology, and tools that will be covered in the complete course. This module is suitable for executive audiences as well as the team members who prepare decisions and strategies for executive staff. Main sections include the anatomy of a decision, what is quality in decisions, and what is the relationship between strategy and decisions. Three case studies from actual corporate situations are included. Detailed agenda is as follows:

- ○ Introduction 15
- ○ Distinctions between strategic and operational management 15
- ○ A simple risky decision problem 45
- ○ Case example: Human Monoclonal Antibodies 30
- ○ Case example: Blackgold Petroleum 15
- ○ Break 15
- ○ Building quality into strategic decisions 45
- ○ What is a good strategy and how do you develop one? 20
- ○ Case example: High-definition TV strategy development 30
- ○ Conclusions and discussion 10

  —This module is essential for everyone, including senior leaders/ decision owners.

2. Framing Strategic Decisions—this module covers framing, creating a solid foundation for good decisions, and strategies. Framing clarifies the purpose, scope, and perspective of decisions. Thoughtful framing helps avoid many of the most fundamental errors in decision making. Key tools covered are decision analysis cycle, strategic challenges, decision hierarchy, business model, strategy tables, and influence diagrams.

    —This module is especially valuable for strategy and marketing people.

3. Alternative Generation and Business Design—this module expands upon Module 2, exploring business model design in depth and exploring methods and tools for developing strategic alternatives. Key tools covered are generic profit models, generic business models, levels of strategic control, and further skill building with strategy tables.

    —This module is especially valuable for strategy and marketing people.

4. Evaluating Decisions and Strategies under Uncertainty—this module starts with the design of decision-focused (spreadsheet) models for ease of deterministic sensitivity analysis, probabilistic (risk) analysis, and decision tree analysis. The role of influence diagrams as blueprints for model building is discussed. Key tools covered are decision

models, empirical market share rules, empirical market penetration curves, and sensitivity tornado charts.

—This module is especially relevant for financial analysts and optional for strategists.

5. Probability Assessment—this module focuses on how to elicit valid information on uncertain critical variables from subject matter experts. The encoding process will be demonstrated, and then participants will practice their techniques. Key tools are the probability encoding interview process, structuring, judgment de-biasing techniques, and entering probabilistic data into Crystal Ball and decision trees.

—This module is relevant for both financial analysts and strategists, but not absolutely essential. Very useful for marketing and research and development.

6. Decision Criteria, Metrics, Probabilistic Analysis, and Expected Value—this module focuses on how to evaluate and recommend the "best" alternative in an uncertain decision/strategy situation. Key tools discussed are financial metrics (net present value (NPV), economic value added (EVA), return on investment (ROI), Shareholder Value Added), decision criteria (Expected Value, Certain Equivalent), Monte Carlo analysis, and decision tree analysis.

—This module is an advanced topic and will not be presented.

7. Putting it all together: Excellence in Strategy Development—this module covers how to manage a strategy development effort and how to present the results. Key tools are the dialogue decision process and hybrid strategy analysis.

—This module is very useful for everyone, including management.

8. Putting it all together: Value-Based Portfolio Management—this module covers how to design and conduct a portfolio management process and how to present the results. Key tools include strategic alignment techniques, risk-return plots, portfolio optimization, and efficient frontier analysis.

—This module is very useful for everyone, including management.

Useful Information (Diagrams, Exhibits, And Text) for Building Your CPM Business Case

This section contains information that may be useful to you in developing your business case. If you would like to have a soft copy of any of these, email me at asanwal@corporateportfoliomanagement.org.

Useful Quote

[T]he notion that a large multi-unit firm must be managed strategically and financially as a portfolio of business strategies with different opportunities, risks, and cash flows is at the heart of modern effective resource management. Systems to achieve this kind of direction and control can be found at the heart of virtually every well-run company.

Joseph L. Bower, Harvard Business School

What we see/hear today	CPM philosophy	How do we enable this?
Decibel-driven decisions —"I know what my business needs" —How loud does one yell? —Who do you know? —Who gave the best presentation?	"If it is not being measured, it is not being managed." —*famous business axiom*	• Robust modeling to understand financial strategic, risk, and so on costs and benefits • Understand key performance indicators (business drivers) to model the "right things"—measuring wrong things is useless
Not fully utilizing in-house experience —"We don't have time to look back. We are managing our business for the future."	"Those who cannot learn from history are doomed to repeat it." —*George Santayana*	• Utilize historical results to help improve future year projections • Leverage this historical learning to resource allocation
Exogenous factors used to explain misses —"The project was going well until ____ stepped in or until ____ happened."	"Accountability breeds response-ability." —*Stephen Covey*	• Investment tracking on an ongoing basis lets decision makers identify bad projects before it's too late • Increased data around initiatives forces greater accountability
Silo approach to allocation —"My business needs this money to achieve our goals." —"I have too many good projects and too little money within my own world."	"Pursue goals that best serve the organization." —*Jack Welch*	• Provide a discipline that can be used by decision makers to optimize their own portfolio of investments • Aggregate these portfolios to arrive at an enterprise-wide optimized portfolio • A meritocratic method to allocate resources
The annual performance trap —"This investment was approved at the beginning of the year and so the money is ours to spend as we see fit."	"Innovation is stifled by rigid adherence to fixed plans and resource allocations agreed to 12 to 18 months earlier." —*Jeremy Hope*	• Investments are "alive" and treated as such • Get rid of annual performance contract to allow flexibility to cut or increase investment spending as performance dictates

EXHIBIT A.2   DATA IS AT THE HEART OF CPM, BUT IT'S ONLY THE START

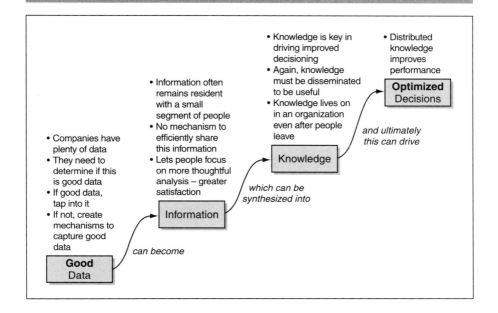

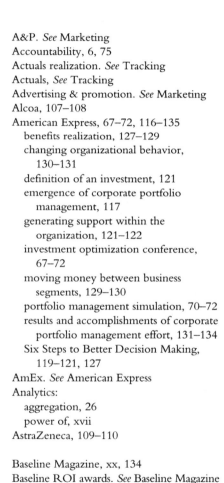